Lighthouses of En

LIZARD POINT

by

Martin Boyle

B&T Publications

Published by B & T Publications
10 Orchard Way . Highfield . Southampton
Hampshire . England SO17 1RD UK

Copyright © 1999 Martin Boyle,
who is the recognised author of this work
in accordance with Section 77 of the Copyright,
Designs and Patents Act 1988

All rights reserved. No part of this publication
may be reproduced or transmitted in any form
or by any means, electronic or mechanical;
photocopying, recording, or any storage and
retrieval system, without the permission of the
Copyright holder.

International Standard Book Number

ISBN 1901043134

International Standard Serial Number

ISSN 1363 8009

Typesetting by mjb graphics

Lighthouses of Cornwall & Isles of Scilly

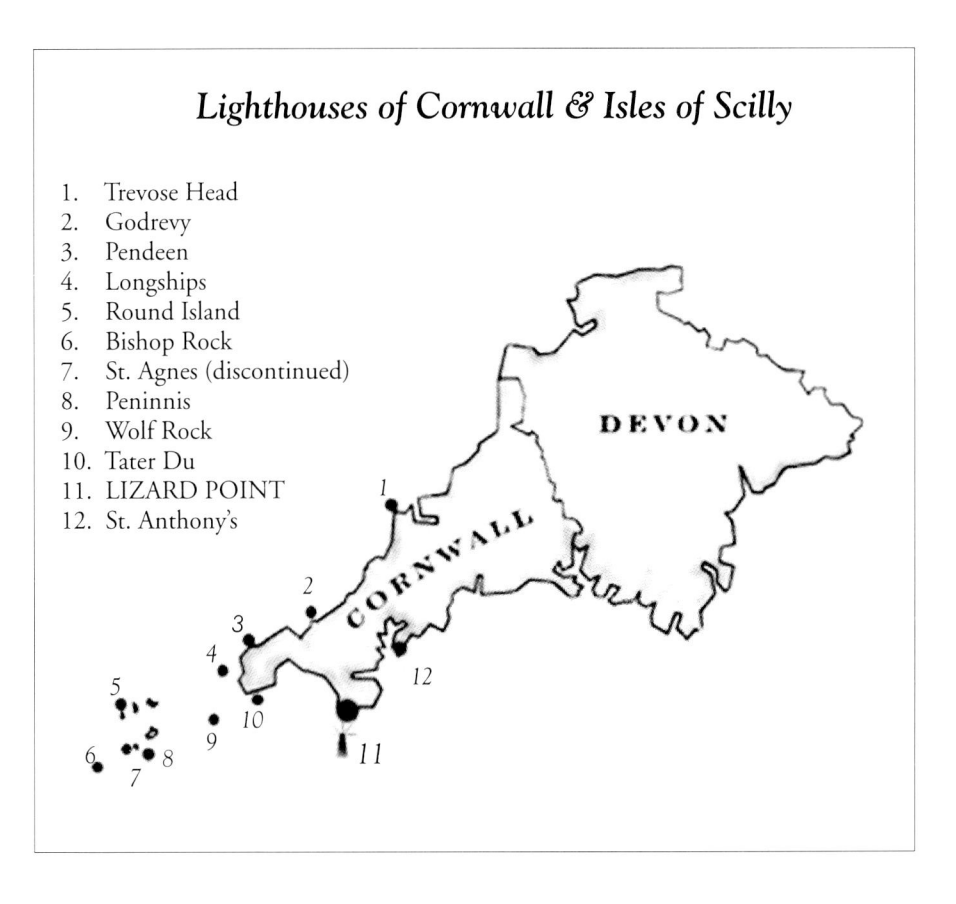

1. Trevose Head
2. Godrevy
3. Pendeen
4. Longships
5. Round Island
6. Bishop Rock
7. St. Agnes (discontinued)
8. Peninnis
9. Wolf Rock
10. Tater Du
11. LIZARD POINT
12. St. Anthony's

SPECIAL ACKNOWLEDGMENT

The author gratefully acknowledges the invaluable help of the Corporation of Trinity House, its Publications Officer and Media Director. Its Director of Engineering and his exceptional staff, with the full cooperation of its Master and Elder Brethren.

CONTENTS

6.	Graveyard of Ships
6.	First Letter Patent -Pirates
8.	The Marie
8.	Virtual Bankrupt
9.	Grandson-Sir John Killigrew the Second
9.	Loss of Treasure Ship-Letter Patent Renewed
10.	Hostile Local People-Squadron of Dragoons
10.	Lizard Point Finally Lit
12.	Light Extinguished
13.	For as long as ye both shall live
14.	Trinity House & Admiral Sir William Monson
16.	Accusation of Piracy
18.	New Petition for Lizard Light
18.	A Divided Country
19.	An Ill Informed Committee
20.	Not a Promontory, Island or Rock
22.	Captain Farish & Thomas Fonnereau
24.	Specifications of the Lizard Lighthouses
26.	Extra Clauses Disputed in Lease.
26.	High Court Ruling
27.	Act of Parliament Required for Oil Lamps
29.	Not During Divine Worship
29.	Family Status Quarters
30.	Cherubim & Ocean Queen
31.	Lizard Lifeboat and the Czar
32.	Discovery of Sir Michael Faraday
35.	Brightest Lights Around England & Powerful Fog Siren
37.	Loss of the Suffolk
38.	Only One Light Required
39.	A World at War (1914-18)
40.	Refrigerator Ship Bardic
40.	A New Light Source
41.	An Air Borne War
41.	Tell Them I'm Polishing the Lantern Glass
42.	Connected to National Power Grid
43.	Lives of the Keepers
49.	The Final Days Automation
54.	Reference Sources & Acknowledgments
55.	Notifications
56.	Further Reading -Book Club Details -Pharos Pen Pal Club

Reproduced with kind permission of Trinity House

LIZARD POINT

POSITION: 49 57'06" N 05 12'01" W
LOCATION: Between Falmouth & Penzance South West Cornwall
NO. ON ADMIRALTY LIST OF LIGHTS: 0060
TOWERS CONSTRUCTED: 24th May 1750 15th July 1751
DESIGNERS & BUILDER: Captain J. Cartert & Captain E. Smith Thomas Fonnereau
COMPOSITION OF STRUCTURES: Octagonal granite masonry
HEIGHT OF TOWERS FOUNDATION TO GALLERY: (both) 61ft (18.6m)
FOCAL PLANE OF LIGHTS: (west) 229ft (69.8m) (east) 232ft (70.7m) *AHWST*
LIGHTS FIRST LIT: 15th July 1752
AUTOMATED DEMANNED: 16th July 1998
MONARCH AT TIME OF MAIN CONSTRUCTION: George 11 (16831760)

AHWST Above high water spring tides (Old Terminology)

Lizard Point

Graveyard of Ships

On the heel of South Cornwall, is the massive headland of Lizard Point. Its notoriety derives from being one of the most treacherous mariners nightmares around the coast of England. Even on a calm summers day the Atlantic rollers pound their way into the rugged cliffs in spectacular fashion. During the winter the sea literally smashes into this jagged shoreline, sending its spray cascading over the summit of Lizard Point like heavy rain. The cliffs around this area rise to over 170 ft (*52 m*) above sea level.

To the east of the Point is the *'Devil's Frying Pan'*, where the sea froths when it washes across this circular under water hollow. West of the promontory is the *'Devil's Bellows'*, where the waves rush into a cavern and erupt into clouds of spray, as it forces a way through a large fissure in the granite headland.

A view of St. Michael's Mount from Marazion. Author's collection.

Up to the 14th century the only recognised *'guiding light'* was the coal burning chaldron established on top of the chapel of St. Michael's Mount. This fortress style monastery was erected on this island in Mounts Bay and provided a navigational reference for ships serving the Papal Order. However it was never intended for this light to be for shipping in general, yet when utlised it proved to be very advantageous to the local fishermen.

It is therefore not surprising that Lizard Point became the first site for a planned maritime light, especially with its reputation as the *'Graveyard of Ships'*.

First Letter Patent-Pirates

The history of the Lizard light begins during the 16th century and its owner Sir John Killigrew. This knight of the realm obtained a Royal Letter Patent from Elizabeth I in 1570, for the erection of a navigation light on his land at Lizard Point. But when considering he headed a family that was engaged in privateering, smuggling, piracy and the plundering of wrecked ships, his motive for such a venture seems questionable. His brazen attitude regarding these activities, saw him not only funding the escapades of the west country pirates, but often accommodating them at his mansion home of Arwenack House. [4]

In 1557 Sir John Killigrew and his pirates seized a Spanish galleon as she rounded Land's End. Her cargo of silver bullion was valued at £10,000. Under the guise of *'legalised privateering'*, he paid his 20% duty to the Royal Treasury and retained the remaining fortune. Sir John was then considered philanthropic by the local people, when most of the bullion was used to finance the building of new houses and roads around Falmouth harbour. Much of Arwenack House is reported to be built from the proceeds of piracy. [4]

But Sir John's status in the community was his grand position as Vice Admiral for Cornwall and the Captain-in-Chief of Pendennis Castle.

At the Royal court Sir John Killigrew was not looked upon as a pirate, but a loyal subject of Queen Mary I. His activities clearly provided the *'Privy Purse'* with a steady income. Many west country noblemen were eager to finance his ventures which often trebled their original investment. His organising skills encompassed much of the Cornish coast line, an area from which he hired men and ships. When these vessels returned from their plundering sorties, Sir John openly sold the proceeds and arranged the movement of any smuggled goods around every part of Cornwall. Even the *'revenue men'* or Customs Officers accepted the money from Sir John as part of their terms of employment.

The cleverest move by Sir John Killigrew in 1559 was to influence Elizabeth I into making him the Commissioner for Piracy in Cornwall. His mandate required him to seek out these *'undesirables'* and bring them to justice. In this exalted position no one questioned why he regularly mixed with known pirates in the taverns. [5]

It would therefore seem that Sir John Killigrew was liked by everyone in the Royal court, but in fact this was not the case. The Lord Lieutenant for the West Country, Edmund Tremayne and his associate, the Clerk of the Privy Council, Sir Richard Grenville, were strongly opposed to the activities of this knight of the realm. From numerous discussions with French and Spanish ambassadors, it was clear that the actions of Sir John were effecting the relationship between the three countries. However, it appeared that this *'Royal favourite'* had the full blessing of the Queen, which made it virtually impossible for anyone to discredit him. Sir John covered his tracks meticulously and ensured his activities were well organised, with suitable bribes paid or violence carried out by his henchmen. Therefore little or no evidence could be found to incriminate him.

A ship owned by Sir John Killigrew returned to Falmouth in September 1569 carrying plunder from its latest venture. As the vessel came into harbour the pirates on board were confronted by a squadron of English warships. A Master, Captain Jones, recognised the ship as one he tried to apprehend near the French coast a few days earlier. But when Captain Jones and his boarding party approached the moored vessel, they were intercepted by Sir John Killigrew. After a short conversation between the two men, the Officer accepted a bribe of one hundred pounds to ignore the ship. Yet there was one person which Sir John had no control over and that was his wife.

****

The Marie

Lady Killigrew supported her husband's activities even to the point of going on some of the raids with his pirates. But greed became her downfall following the arrival of the 144 ton Spanish merchant ship *Marie*. During a lull in the war between England and Spain, the *Marie* sought refuge in Falmouth harbour after a severe storm. While repairs were being carried out during January 1583 her owners, Juan de Chaves and Philip de Orio, accepted the hospitality of Sir John at Arwenack House.

On the 8th January Lady Killigrew plus several pirates from Penryn and members of her household, seized the *Marie* and sailed her out of Falmouth. Even the duty officer at Pendennis Castle was bribed to ensure the ship could leave port unharmed. When the ship was ten miles out to sea her skeleton crew were thrown over board by the pirates. A course was then set for Roaring Bay in Ireland, where within two days of arriving, the *Marie* and her cargo was sold. Once the proceeds were divided between Lady Killigrew and the pirates, they all split up and made their way back to Cornwall.

The owners of the *Marie* lodged a formal complaint with Sir John Killigrew, but although numerous people were questioned by the militia nothing was found. However the two Spaniards were not satisfied at the way the investigation was handled and reported the matter to the Earl of Bedford and Edmund Tremayne. This news was welcomed by these two men who took the opportunity to intervene, especially as it finally gave them a chance to discredit the Killigrew family.

Under intense interrogation a Falmouth tavern owner, Elizabeth Moore, admitted lying to the original investigators and that two men, Henry Kendal and John Hawkins, were not at her inn when the *Marie* went missing. When the men were questioned in Pendennis Castle, they confessed to being among the pirates. But in an attempt to gain their freedom they implicated Lady Killigrew as the leader. At last Edmund Tremayne, Sir Richard Grenville and the Earl of Bedford, had enough evidence to destroy Sir John's credibility in the Royal Court.

Using his power as Lord Lieutenant of Cornwall, Edmund Tremayne ordered the arrest of the accomplices and prosecuted them at the Launceston assizes. In April 1583 Hawkins, Kendal and Lady Killigrew were found guilty and sentenced to death for piracy. [5]

Virtual Bankrupt

Sir John Killigrew was devastated at the outcome of the court case and openly stated that his wife had been falsely accused in a conspiracy instigated by his enemies. On the grounds of a miscarriage of justice he lodged an appeal to the Royal court of Elizabeth I, through his friends, Sir John Arundell and Sir Nicholas Hals. His cousin, William Killigrew a groom in the Queen's household, obtained a pardon for Lady Killigrew just hours before she was due to be executed. However mercy pleas for Hawkins and Kendal were rejected. On the 25th May 1583 they were executed and their bodies left hanging outside of the Launceston court house for three days, with the intention of deterring acts of piracy. [4]

When the news of Lady Killigrew's pardon reached other west country pirates, they refused to be involved with any more of Sir John's privateering missions. In 1584 Sir John tried to sell his Patent for the Lizard light, but no one took up the option. With no light being established he surrendered his rights to the Privy Council. Two months later Sir John died a virtual bankrupt and heavily in debt to the sum of £10,000, the amount it cost him to secure his wife's release. [12]

Grandson-Sir Killigrew the Second

At the beginning of the 17th century Sir John Killigrew's grandson restored the family's fortunes to their former glory. However this was from his barbaric acts of smuggling and wrecking. Also named Sir John, he formed his own militia which closely guarded all of the coastal regions around his Cornish lands. In turn these thugs took control of any ship that was wrecked and commandeered all the cargoes under custom and descent. Anyone refusing to cooperate were beaten mercilessly or killed. Even the law of the time recognised Sir John's rights, which stated he was entitled to any salvage found on his land. [12]

The stretch of coastline from Coverjack to Porthleven and around the deadly Manacles Reef, was the Killigrew's prime wrecking site. One of the most profitable was Kynance Cove, where during the winter months at least one ship each week was being wrecked. As the Lord of the Manor Sir John enjoyed his 60% share of the plunder, with the Crown turning a blind eye at his activities because of the 20% dividend paid into the Royal Treasury. The balance of the plunder was shared between the wrecking community.

Loss of Treasure Ship-Letter Patent Renewed

In 1619 a ship carrying a fortune in bullion was lost near Lizard Point. The major portion of her cargo was recovered by Sir John Killigrew and his divers, with the customary Royalty share paid into the Privy purse of King James I. Sir John decided this would be the ideal time to pursue the Lizard light Patent, by using the loss of this important ship as the prime reason for its renewal. He contacted his cousin, Sir Dudley Carleton, the Ambassador for Holland and asked him to use his influence for this venture. He also promised to share with him the expected lucrative profits from a navigation light. [12]

Sir Dudley Carleton (*later Lord Dorchester*) was a close friend and business associate of the Lord High Admiral, the Duke of Buckingham. As the King's favourite it was a mere formality for the Duke to obtain permission for the proposed Lizard Point light.

On the 29th June 1619 the Letter Patent for the light was issued to Sir John Killigrew and his builder partner Robert Thynne. It authorised the establishing of the Lizard light for a period of 50 years and without any *'Royal'* rent being required. Instead the Crown stated that Sir John and his partner had to '*erect and maintain the light at their own expense'*, as a charitable act for the mariner. Erection of any other lights along the south coast of Cornwall was forbidden. The Elder Brethren of Trinity House fiercely opposed the petition, on the grounds that the '*English Channel being so deep and good,*' made the site free of any outlying dangers. The main objection stated that the Lizard light would '*assist pirates and the King's enemies who might desireth a suitable landfall'*. The outcome of these objections brought about an unexpected clause in the Letter Patent, which deleted the '*compulsory dues*' from shipping, to '*voluntary contributions*'. Sir John and his partner naively believed that this would not be a problem, especially with the number of Shipowners and Masters who had supported his application and promised to pay for its upkeep. [12]

Hostile Local People - Squadron of Dragoons

Within a week of receiving their Letter Patent Sir John and his partner Robert Thynne began building the Lizard lighthouse. But by the end of the month a mob of local people had attacked the workers and destroyed the partly built structure. By the end of August the same year Sir John could not find any local builders who would work on the project. They claimed the light was going to take away their winter income from wrecked ships. When workers were drafted in from Bodmin or Truro, the nearby wrecking community came to the site in force with three of the builders killed. Once more the partly completed tower was razed to the ground. [4]

By September Sir John and Robert Thynne were forced to write to Lord Dorchester and tell him that the Lizard light was seriously delayed. They also complained about the barbaric actions of the local people. In his letter Sir John wrote: '*I assure your Lordship, yt hath byn more chargeable and far more trobellsom than I expected for the inabytants near yt think they suffer yn this erection. They affirm I take awaye God's Grace from them. Their english meanin ys that they no longer shall receive no more beyfitt by shipwrack (for this lyght will prevent yt). They have been so long used to repe by the Callamyte of the Ruin of Shipping as they clayme yt Heredytorye, and hourly complayne on me. Costom breeds strange ylls......but I hope they wyll now husband theyr Land, whych theyr former idell Lyfee hath omitted in assurance of theyr gayne by shipwarck.* [12]

Within a week of receiving the letter from Sir John Killigrew, the Duke of Buckingham ordered a squadron of dragoons to protect the Lizard Point site. These soldiers were instructed to shoot anyone who interfered with the project or any of the workers, on the direct orders of King James I.

Lizard Point Finally Lit

Very few records have survived which give a true representation of what the original tower looked like. But from the details of its size and specifications noted in the Guildhall Library records, the talents of Barry Hawkins (*former assistant keeper*) have been utilised to portray an assumed likeness. It is understood that the wooden lattice style tower was about 40-50 ft (*12-15m*) in height. Its base consisted of granite rubble masonry, formed into a typical Cornish wall construction without the use of mortar. This stonework surround a timber structure which had six legs of oak, which tapered from 20 ft (*6m*) in diameter to its iron decking. This metal section is believed to have been 12 ft (*3.6m*) in diameter, on to which was stood a large fire basket.

Coal which was used to fuel the fire, had to be hauled up in baskets by ropes to the top of the tower. Access to the fire was by means of a series of ladders fixed to the side of the tower. Adjacent to this structure was a small enclosure where the coal was stored and another area for holding the cinders and ash. Accommodation for the keeper and his family consisted of

Artistic impression of the Killigrew lighthouse by Barry Hawkins.

a single storey rubble stone cottage, with a roof covered with thick Cornish slate. This dwelling was situated to the rear of the tower. The whole site was then enclosed in a low level Cornish style rubble masonry wall. [4]

On the 12th December 1619 Sir John Killigrew wrote to Lord Dorchester and informed him about the progress of the venture. He wrote: *'the Light and Tower on Lizard is, I prayse God, finished and I presum speaks ytself to most parts of Christendom....the Light cannot be mentayned under 10sg (ten shillings) a nyght.'* By the beginning of January 1620 Sir John was facing financial ruin, because none of the original Shipowners or Masters who had promised to *'voluntarily contribute'* towards the upkeep of the light had paid. Out of 300 people who had signed his petition only 20 made any payment.

At the end of January 1620 Sir John wrote to his cousin once, Lord Dorchester, in which he complained: *'I protest I am out about thys business 500£, and yet no return....I am now attempting to gett an imposition lyk the Dungenesse and other Lights yn England have, but I dyspair yn yt this time. My misfortunes meet together....Yt must be granted that the Light ys, under God, a Particular Advantage that all shyps shall offten recover theyr owne Ports; by reson that the Light lets them know with assurance wheare they ar, and so they need nott keepe off at sea all night but dyrect theyr course home whych yf they should beate off at sea....can make Land agayne.'* [12]

11

Treacherous coastline below Lizard Point lighthouse. Author's collection.

Light Extinguished

By the late spring of 1620 Sir John Killigrew had written to Lord Dorchester, in which he complained once more about the lack of money and also that none of the *'rutters' (early Admiralty List of Lights and Seamarks)* made any mention of the Lizard light. He wrote: *'a ship had peryshed thro nott havyng noticed that anye such light was there mentayned and the men Drunk, beyng confessed by them that ar saved. I yntreat your LP's (Lordships) speedye resolution whether I shal continue the light or nott for the charge ys so heavy.'* [12]

He continued in his long letter by saying that there were few records which would give any insight to the numbers of ships lost near the Lizard Point, mainly because hardly any mariners survived to report the incident. In fact he was concerned that most of the houses around the area had been built from the proceeds and remains of the numerous ships that were wrecked. His final note commented that the cost of maintaining the light was a very heavy burden and he needed to find £50 to purchase more coal for the following winter months.

However by September 1620 it appears from various records that Sir John Killigrew had extinguished the Lizard light because no one was paying for its upkeep. During the period when the light was not lit, a fleet of ships approaching the Lizard headland were unable to fix their position in the darkness. A lookout in the watchman's cottage noticed the small oil burning lanterns on these vessels and reported the sighting to Sir John Killigrew. On hearing the news he sent one of his cutters with several of his militia on board to intercept the ships. The Commander of the fleet ordered six of his vessels to go on ahead as a means to plot a safe course. Sir John wrote: '*the ships that transported the 8000 soldiers from Lisbon to Dunkirk, looking for the Light (whych I have put out) six of the ships were near perishyng on the Lizard. They expressed theyr joy by dischargyng theyr ordynance for such a delivery.*' [4]

When considering the old version of '*ordinance*' meant '*the art of arranging or to put in order*', it can only be assumed that some form of signalling was made to the remainder of the fleet, that their location was now positively known. Yet some historians have stated that Sir John Killigrew had in fact sequestered sums of money from the Masters of these vessels. If he had in fact done this he would have been in breach of his Letter Patent, which clearly stated that the voluntary contributions could be taken from shipping but: '*other than His Majesty's Ships of War.*' [7]

'For as long as ye both shall live'

Without suitable finances derived from the voluntary contributions, Sir John Killigrew and his partner Robert Thynne formally notified the Duke of Buckingham that they were extinguishing the Lizard light. Their letter was given to the Lord High Admiral by Lord Dorchester at the beginning of November 1620. Over the next two months tremendous gales and storms lashed the Cornish coastline, bringing tragic consequences for passing shipping. At least 25 vessels were reported lost during this six week period and all close to the Lizard headland. Most the ships could not be positively identified because all of the wreckage, flotsam, cargo and bodies, was all mixed together in one confined area. For the local wrecking community it was a '*gift from God*'.

At the beginning of January 1621 James I personally intervened, after hearing about the tragic events from the Lords of the Privy Council. Certain influential people in the Royal court wanted the King to arrest Sir John and his partner, because they believed it was their fault that the tragedy had occurred due to the light being extinguished. But because the light was still classed as a charitable aid to mariners, there was no formal legal binding contract which stated Sir John had to keep the light lit. He only had the King's blessing and right to collect voluntary contributions. It was clearly up to the partners if they continued to show a light.

King James however, decided to send a special Royal courier with a letter carrying the Royal Seal, which ordered Sir John and Robert Thynne to relight the Lizard light. The Duke of Buckingham was also ordered to contact the Shipowners and Masters who had signed the original petition and to give them the incentive to make the necessary voluntary contributions. But in reality nothing further was done to change the upkeep clause for another two years. [12]

During this 24 month period many Shipowners and Masters did feel inclined to pay towards the upkeep of the Lizard light, but a large proportion of the money collected by the Customs Officers at various ports of destination rarely reached Sir John or his partner. On the 16th September 1623 friends of Sir John, namely Sir Francis Godolphin and Sir Anthony Harris, wrote to the Privy Council to inform '*their Lordships*' that the majority of the Shipowners and Masters fully supported the need for the Lizard Point light. Yet those from many Cornish ports such as Penryn did not. During the previous six months, prior to the letter being drafted, it was calculated that only '*£13*' had been received by Sir John or his partner. With the upkeep of the light costing '*ten shillings*' a night, Sir John and Robert Thynne had spent '*£91*', with a loss in revenue of '*£78*'.

Sir Francis Godolphin also informed the Lords of the Privy Council, that investigations into the non payment towards the Lizard light by the Shipowners and Masters from Melcome Regis and Weymouth had been completed. The outcome was that the Customs Officers reported that these mariners felt the light to be: '*needless and more dangerous than profitable to shipping in hazy weather*'. In clear weather they stated that the land was often seen before the light. However if the light dues had been made compulsory at least '*£20*' would have been collected over the previous six months from just the Weymouth shipping. In real terms all that was collected amounted to '*£1 1s 4d*', or enough to maintain the light for two nights.

By the middle of October 1623 Lord Dorchester had received several letters from the Newfoundland fishermen, who complained about the unfair and extremely high levy being imposed by many Customs Officers for the upkeep of the Lizard light. When further enquiries were made it was found that none of the money ever reached Sir John or Robert Thynne. Agents for the Privy Council investigated this possible misappropriation of money, but no action was taken against the Customs Officers. It was decided that as no receipts were issued and no record kept of the ships concerned, there was not enough proof to substantiate the alleged fraud.

On the 14th November 1623 James I ordered that: '*the Tower or Lighthouse should remain a Lighthouse for ever on that coast*' and he also granted Sir John and his partner Robert Thynne, the right to exhibit a light from Lizard Point: '*for as long as ye both shall live.*' This new clause in the Letter Patent even clarified that the rights applied to the longest life span of either person. However, based upon a document which falsely represented the income received by Sir John and his partner, a rent was imposed at '*£40*' per year. Trinity House was accused at this time of being the main cause of this confusion. Its financial committee estimated that the voluntary contributions paid at '*one half penny per tun*', had provided the Patentees with a '*£400*' net profit for 1623. This information misled James I and caused him to retain the voluntary clause in the Letter Patent. This obviously upset Sir John and Robert Thynne. [7]

Trinity House & Admiral Sir William Monson

By the end of December 1623 the Elder Brethren of Trinity House were openly condemning the Lizard Point light. In a letter sent to the Privy Council on the 12th December, the Corporation stated that the light was totally unnecessary and with the '*road being so broad*' (*English Channel*), very few ships actually saw the light. Also it had become an unwarranted burden on shipping to pay the so called voluntary contribution towards its upkeep. [6]

Admiral Sir William Monson, a close friend of Sir John Killigrew and also a member of the Privy Council, reminded '*their Lordships*' on the 4th February 1624, that the King had

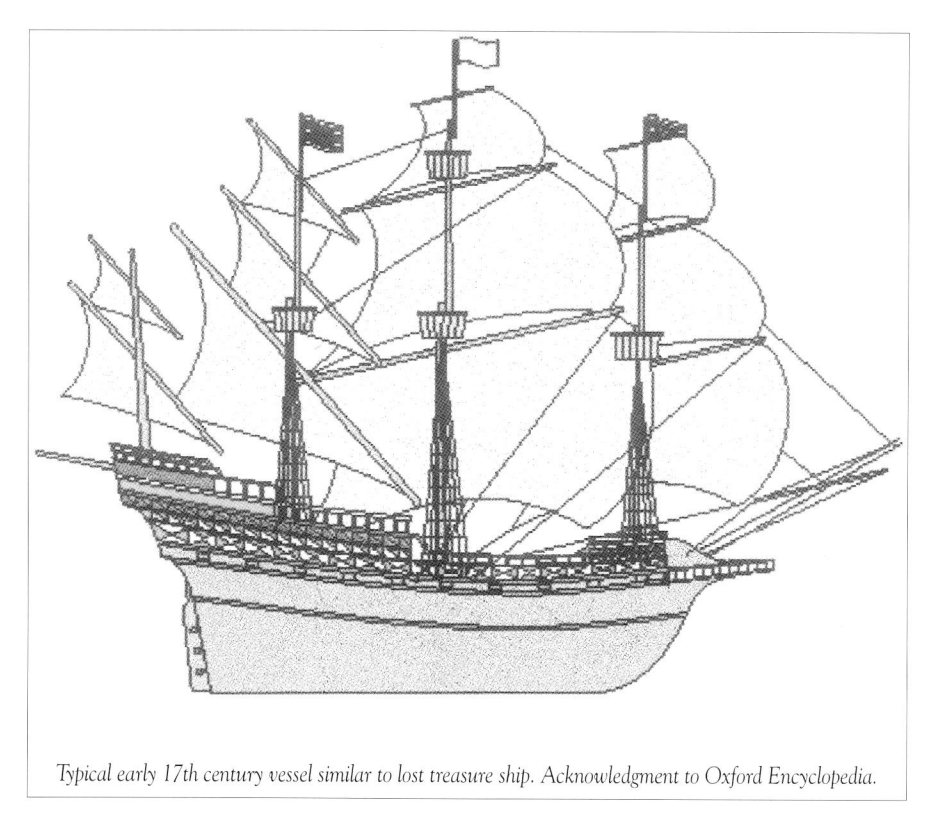

Typical early 17th century vessel similar to lost treasure ship. Acknowledgment to Oxford Encyclopedia.

declared the importance of the Lizard light. From his drafted speech taken out of the documents and letters held in the Parliamentary Archives, he stated: '*It is most fitt seamen should be furnished with as manie other helps as can be devised. There is noe man that hath layne tossing at sea some tyme but will be glad to make land, for a good landfall is the principall thinge to find cominge for our coast....what a comfort a shipp in distress shall find by this light, it is to be imagined by example of a traveller on land losinge his waie in a dark cold night, and discerning a light in a cottage or hearinge a ringe of bells, by reason of which he maie be directed.*' [4]

This very long speech included a statement that since the Lizard light had been established, the Dutch had willingly contributed towards its upkeep and along with numerous English warships, they had reduced the number of pirate around the Cornish coast. In particular those pirate vessels which were using the Lizard light to bring their plunder or smuggled goods ashore, or for their crews to obtain provisions. The Admiral praised the Lizard light for so many different reasons, although some were nothing to do with it at all. It was obvious that the light was providing a major service, not only for warning shipping away from the treacherous Cornish coast, but as a guide for vessels trying to find a safe haven.

Admiral Sir William Monson concluded his speech by finally getting to the main reason for the statement to the Lords of the Privy Council, with a reference to the dire need to change the voluntary payment clause to compulsory. He said: *'Divers other misfortunes I could collect together with the fearfull wracks that have been in Mounts Baye, which is sufficient to prove the necessarie convenience of a Light to be placed on the Promentarie of the Lizard, if it be carefully preserved and maintayned with fewell as I am informed it nowe is.'* [4]

Trinity House still continued its campaign of condemning the Lizard light and insisting that its use was a guide to the Kings enemies at a time of war. Also numerous Customs Officers still believed they could put the money due to Sir John Killigrew and his partner, to much better use with very little of the levy ever reaching the Patentees. During the latter part of spring 1624 Sir John Killigrew and Robert Thynne surrendered their rights for the Lizard light. They stated in the letter to the Privy Council, that it was an expensive folly. [7]

Accusation of Piracy

Although the Killigrew fortunes took an upward trend, those people who were unable to share in the rich pickings from the ships being wrecked, decided to instigate a campaign to undermine Sir John's power. Within three years complaints were received by the Privy Council, which condemned the Killigrew family for exploiting the rights of custom and descent. These letters openly stated that what was happening amounted to heartless plundering and piracy.

On the 9th March 1627 Captain John Mason, an experienced diver and his merchant business partner Jacob Johnson, filed a complaint to the Privy Council. They claimed that over the past eight years their investigations had shown that Sir John Killigrew had ordered his men to force a ship on to the rocks close to Lizard Point. This statement referred to a Dutch ship which was enroute to its home port of St. Lucar in 1619. It reported that this vessel had a cargo of *'pieces of eight'* and numerous ingots of silver. A further claim stated that information had been given to Sir John by informers in Bristol about the movements of this ship. In turn he had ordered two of his cutters to intercept the vessel as she came into the English Channel.

When the ship was wrecked on the rocks near Lizard Point, Sir John's men threatened to kill the survivors if they attempted to hinder any salvage operation. Because of this barbaric act, Captain Mason and Jacob Johnson requested the intervention of the Duke of Buckingham to formally investigate the incident. They also asked that the proceeds from the wreck already recovered, should be returned to its owners with Sir John Killigrew arrested for piracy.

In response to these *'wild'* accusations Sir John wrote to the Duke of Buckingham, in which he acknowledged the loss of the vessel in question. In fact he was very explicit with his description of the ship and the value of its cargo. When referring to the subsequent salvage operation, he wrote: *'of wch I desyr nott to be called to account, although on that land priscription hath made my forefathers demand yt, and I have nott lost the right wch custom and descent gave me.'* He finally asked the Duke of Buckingham to check through the official Treasury Papers for that period. [12]

When this item was investigated the Duke found details of the vessel concerned, plus a copy of a receipt given to Sir John Killigrew for a share of the silver. Attached to these documents was another letter from Sir John to his cousin Lord Dorchester, in which he stated: '*silver bars worth £3,300 have been salvaged from a Dutch ship, wch His Highness hath received.*'

Another letter was sent to the Duke of Buckingham from Sir John Killigrew, in which he stated that all of the surviving Dutch crew were drunk. Also none of them were anywhere near the wreck site because they had abandoned the vessel. When the ship went on to the rocks his men had risked their lives to salvage what they could for the King. His letter gave the ship's last known location and the information relating to a vast fortune in silver still on board. Yet the final part of the letter read: '*wch nowe ys beyonde reach.*' Although the Duke of Buckingham ordered a team of divers to go to this location the vessel could not be found. However, during these early times this situation was not considered to be unusual. With the atrocious conditions around Lizard Point, the tides and strong currents often moved sunken ships away from their original locations. Some were even covered by the drifting sands of the sea bed.

Other evidence was collected from many local people, including some of the survivors from the Dutch vessel. But there was nothing to support the barbaric claims from Captain Mason or Jacob Johnson.

There was one piece of evidence which came to light, that related to the unscrupulous methods used by Captain Mason and Jacob Johnson during their free lance salvage operations. A particularly violent situation had arisen near the Needles off the Isle of Wight. On this occasion they sent down their divers to recover the bullion from the wreck of the Campden. But when the local people exercised their right of custom and descent, two of them were drowned and many more seriously injured by the private militia employed by the partnership to guard the site. It was later revealed that Captain Mason and Jacob Johnson were never asked to salvage the cargo from the Campden by her owners. In fact the ship was a vessel owned by the King. [5]

After all the information was presented to the Lords of the Privy Council, the outcome stated that Sir John Killigrew had no charges to answer. Any further accusations were also

King Charles I by Van Dyke.

dismissed as being orchestrated by those who were jealous of Sir John's good fortune.

However when researching through various records held in the Public Record Office in London and documents archived in the Hydrographic Department in Taunton, there is certain references to the lost St. Lucar bullion ship. In 1975 a diving team from Penryn and Weymouth were searching for another ship near Lizard Point. However they were surprised to find the location of the St. Lucar ship more than a mile from its previously assumed location. They also reported that the vessel was in an area not known for many ship wrecks and positioned on the sea bed as if it had been scuttled. On board were numerous ingots of silver and several shattered casks containing *'pieces of eight.'* [2]

New Petition for Lizard Light

In 1630 Sir William Killigrew, the former groom for Queen Elizabeth I, applied for the Lizard Point light Patent. His petition read: *'Tis a thing all seamen desire, but most strongest who wonder by what unjust complaints soe great a benefitt is lost. Every year many shippes are wreckt for want of it. I am at the intreaty of all men desired to sett it up againe.'* His other request was to ensure that the light dues were made compulsory for all ships which passed within 15 nautical miles of the light in either direction. The rate proposed was to be *'one half penny per tun.'* At this point a brief explanation should be provided as to the word TUN. This nautical term referred to large barrels which contained wine or other spirits. When a ship was designed its holds were normally made to the specified sizes for carrying a certain number of barrels.

Trinity House opposed the proposal from Sir William, because its Committee believed it would become an unwarranted financial burden for vessels which did not need a light for sailing up or down the English Channel. Also with a renewed threat of war with Spain and the uncertain political upheavals in the Royal Court the application was rejected. [5]

A Divided Country

Any thoughts about lighthouses around the coast of England and Wales, was the last thing to be considered during the middle of the 17th century. After the death of James I in 1625 many politically minded people believed his son, Charles I, would moderate the power being enforced by the monarchy under its *'Divine Right of Kings'* status. Although there was a *'Parliament'* its role was basically as an advisory body which influenced the monarchs decisions regarding the country. However the seeds of revolt had already been sown by his father, but Charles decided to aggravate the situation even further. Political turmoil saw successive Parliaments opposing the King's orders to raise taxes. By 1629 Charles had dismissed these Parliaments and declared himself the supreme and absolute ruler. His only advisors were his chosen favourites who he formed into a powerful House of Lords.

For nearly ten years England was ruled by the King's decree. But the threat of civil war became a reality in 1639 when Charles I married a staunch Catholic, Henrietta Marie. She influenced Charles to try to enforce the Papal Order on the Church of England. He ordered that Archbishop Laud's Anglican prayer book had to be adopted by the Presbyterian

Church in Scotland. For twelve months the '*Bishops*' took up arms and raised their own armies to fight in an unnecessary religious war.

By November 1640 Charles I and his Bishops had suffered a total military defeat at the hands of the Scottish Presbyterians. On his return to London the King ordered the arrest of five members of the newly formed '*Parliament*' on the charge of treason. Yet these former loyal subjects of the King had only tried to end the war, by refusing to allow further money to be taken from the treasury, to pay '*for a War of no Consequences.*' When the so called '*Long Parliament*', which had lasted for three years, opposed the King's order and secreted the Members out of the country, Charles raised his standard. On the 22nd August 1642 the whole of England became a divided nation as its people became embroiled in tragic civil war.

Oliver Cromwell (1599-1658)

For a further three years thousands of men and women died in often futile battles, until in 1645 the two opposing forces met at Naseby. This final battle was the decisive turning point in the war, which saw Charles surrendering to the Scots in February 1646. By the following January he was handed over to the English Parliamentary forces headed by Oliver Cromwell. But while he was under house arrest his supporters managed to free him. He was then taken to the Isle of Wight. With this Island predominately Catholic Charles tried to enlist the help of the Scots to overthrow the English Parliament. Instead the Islanders had seen enough of this tragic war and by the end of 1648 the King was under arrest in the Tower of London. He was later found guilty of High Treason and beheaded on the 30th January 1649. [7]

An Ill Informed Committee

The years between 1649 & 1660 England was run by '*the Rump Parliament*', which was made up of the remnants of '*Church appointed people and ex-military*' personnel. But in 1653 this Parliament was dissolved by Oliver Cromwell, a much respected soldier and statesman of the times. Yet his rise to fame as a political figure head only happened because of his military record and the powerful status achieved through numerous battles. More importantly he formed the New Model Army in 1644 which religiously followed his puritanical doctrines.

When the Rump Parliament was in session it appointed Oliver Cromwell as its Lord Lieutenant of Ireland. Within twelve months his heartless army had suppressed the Irish rebellion and in 1651 he quelled a Royalist uprising of the Scots at Worcester.

One of his first commands as the Lord Protector or Commonwealth President, *(a title he declared himself to be in 1653)* was to dissolve any groups of people or administrations which contained Royalist sympathisers. This action included the Master Mariners of Trinity House who were replaced by an ill informed and relatively useless committee. Any talk of petitions for maritime lights were rejected even from the staunch supporters of Oliver Cromwell. With Britain now under the grips of a self appointed dictator war seemed to be the only policy, with Spain being the prime target for the English forces.

When Oliver Cromwell died in 1658 his son Richard reluctantly took over the position as head of state. But within a year he had cleverly influenced Parliament into considering the restoration of the monarchy. The exiled son of Charles I, namely Charles II, was invited by the English Parliament to leave Holland and to restore the country to its previous Royal status. One of the prime reasons why this decision was made, came from the willingness of Charles to establish a formal Parliament. He also wanted to free the monarchy from its financial dependence on the tax payer. In 1660 Charles II rode unopposed into London to be proclaimed the King of England, Ireland, Scotland & Wales.

Not a Promontory, Island or Rock

With great pomp and ceremony Charles II took up his place in history as the colourful King of Britain. The population found a new meaning for their lives, with peace and a united people being the main goal to strive for. However this turning point in England's history saw many people clamouring towards the modern approach to '*peoples*' power and a very relaxed Royal presence. During the first few years of the new monarchy there was not a promontory, island or off shore rock, that the entrepreneurs of the Royal court were not trying to establish maritime lights upon.

In 1661 Captain Edward Penruddock, *(who was previously involved with General Monk, the bodyguard of the King during his return to England)* applied for a comprehensive Letter Patent to cover the establishment of numerous lights around the coast of England. But the newly reformed Trinity House under the Patronage of Charles II, opposed the proposal on the grounds that the lights were not for shipping in general.

Three years later Sir John Coryton petitioned the Privy Council for Trade to establish lights on Lizard Point and on the Isle of Wight. His applications were backed by numerous Shipowners, Masters and Merchants, who supported the venture based upon a light levy of *'six pence sterling per laden ton.'* It was stated that these dues would only be paid by shipping using the area of sea between Mounts bay in Cornwall to the Isle of Wight.

Yet these petitions came up against a great deal of opposition, especially from the Irish, Scottish and Welsh mariners. In a letter dated the 19th September 1667 sent to Sir John

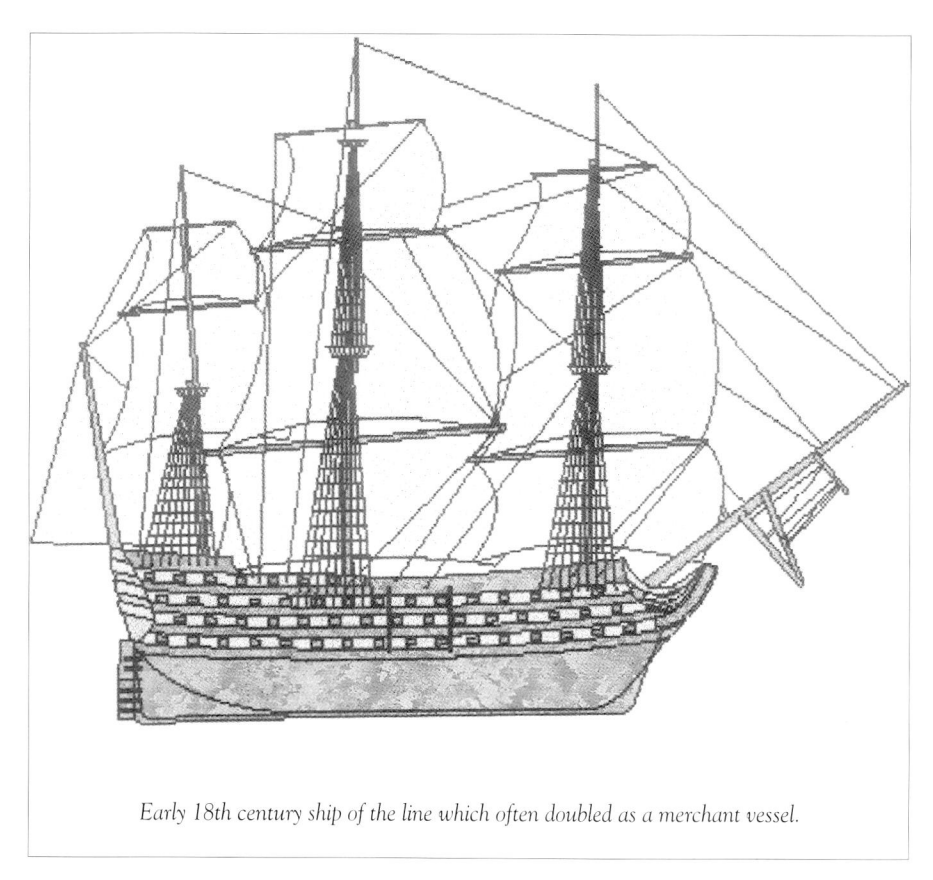

Early 18th century ship of the line which often doubled as a merchant vessel.

Coryton by an influential merchant, Edward Maryford, it stated that the Welsh Shipowners and Masters were petitioning the English Parliament because his proposals classed them as foreign. If this clause was agreed on any Patent, the Welsh mariners would have to pay double the levy for the upkeep of the lights. Fearing a political confrontation and possible rebellion from these very powerful shipping concerns, the Privy Council rejected all of Sir John Coryton's proposals. [11]

There was also a petition sent to the Privy Council in 1669 by a Cornish merchant Henry Brounker. He offered to rebuild the existing tower on the Lizard headland to any specifications laid down by Trinity House. But the very staid Elder Brethren strongly objected to the petition, because they had not been approached in the first place, or given enough time to consider the proposals. Henry Brounker took this objection as a personal insult and withdrew his application. Although contacted by several agents for Trinity House, he refused to communicate with what he stated in his letter as: *'Master Mariners with no heads for business.'* [11]

Captain Farish & Thomas Fonnereau

Civil war had taken its toll on the nobility of England. Also the former servitude attitude of the common folk had changed to one of self preservation. Former claims for coastal salvage rights were difficult to enforce, with these impoverished Cornish people forming themselves into well organised wrecking communities.

The power of the Killigrews had waned, but not totally destroyed by the war. Most of the family members now living in Ireland. Their lands had been over run by the Cromwellian forces, but once more the King restored them to their former status.

However, in 1687 the return to nobility was very short lived, when the last remaining male heir to the family's peerage was killed in a fight at a Penryn tavern. With the Killigrew family now settled in Ireland, there eemed no reason to return. So the lands including Lizard Point were sold to the Crown.

By the latter part of the 17th century there was a dramatic increase in sea trade passing Lizard Point. However this also brought about a rise in ships being wrecked to near epidemic proportions. Plundering and wreck scavenging became common place Most of the local communities would brave the bitterest winter night and wait along the shoreline for their expected rich harvest from the sea. Many of the survivors became second place to the ship's cargo during these barbaric days, with the crew killed to prevent them from making any salvage claim.

In the middle of the 18th century Lizard Point was bought by Thomas Fonnereau, a wealthy merchant from the Channel Islands. With the help of an influential mariner, Captain Richard Farish, a proposal was made to Trinity House for the erection of four lighthouses on the headland.

In September 1748 Captain Farish prepared the petition for the lights, which was supported by numerous local Shipowners and various merchants from the City of London. Other *'memorials'* were provided by the Shipowners of the 'Northern Parts' of England and from Trinity House of Hull. All of these documents were presented to the Corporation of Trinity House of *'Deptford Strond'*, which had the formal authority to sanction the agreement for a new light. [11]

Over the next twelve months consideration was given to the proposals by Captain Farish, but by November 1749 he had been taken seriously ill. To ensure the petition and application remained active Captain Farish changed his will, which formally made Thomas Fonnereau an equal partner in the intended venture. Up to this time Captain Farish was going to lease the headland from Thomas Fonnereau, with him holding the rights to the lights. In this will it specified that on his death, Thomas Fonnereau would be the sole petitioner for the Lizard lights.

In January 1750 Captain Farish died, two months before Trinity House formally consented to the petition. In turn the Corporation applied for its Letter Patent for the lights. On the 9th February 1751 the Lords of the Privy Council of Trade for George II, issued Trinity House with its *'perpetual'* Patent. Negotiations were also finalised with Thomas Fonnereau, regarding his terms for the lease licence of the Lizard Point lights. During this period in the history of Trinity House, it was the policy of the Corporation to

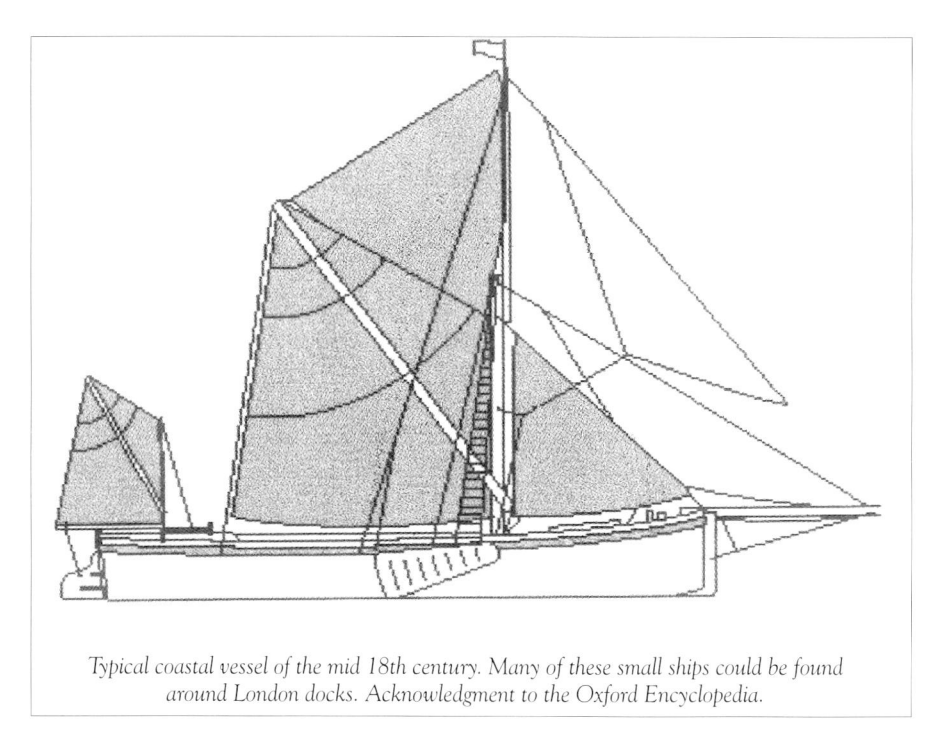

Typical coastal vessel of the mid 18th century. Many of these small ships could be found around London docks. Acknowledgment to the Oxford Encyclopedia.

exploit private ownership of lighthouses even though it held the actual Letter Patent. This system proved far more profitable in the early days of maritime lights around England, with many owners going into bankruptcy because of the number of Shipowners and Masters who did everything they could to avoid paying the light tolls. [11]

When everything seemed settled, Trinity House objected to the proposed four lights and insisted that only two were necessary. It had been the intention of Captain Farish to establish four towers, in the belief that shipping would easily pin point the headland's location both during the day and night. [11]

When levies were imposed the amount due was for each light that the ship passed. However when the Letter Patent was drafted, it clearly stated that the Lizard Point was classed as only one light, irrespective of how many towers were constructed. The lease was issued to Thomas Fonnereau for a period of 61 years at an annual rent of '£80'. As the lessee he was authorised to collect by '*compulsory means*' the sum of '*one halfpenny sterling per laden ton*' from all English ships (*excluding His Majesty's Ships of War*) and double for '*foreign*' vessels. This levy had to be paid for any ship which passed the light in either direction along the English Channel within a 20 miles radius. [7]

The system for collecting the light levy was carried out by the Customs Officers at the ship's port of destination. For those going overseas the levy had to be paid prior to the ship leaving port. However this last item left a lot to be desired as very few records were kept about vessels leaving port. What details were taken seemed to be just for the Customs Officers. It would be another 30 years before formal receipts were issued for the light dues. For this service by the Customs Officers, Thomas Fonnereau paid a fee of 20% of the revenue collected. Every three months the remaining balance was paid to the lessee. Yet something which was to cause a degree of friction between the Corporation and Thomas Fonnereau, was the wording of the Letter Patent. It clearly stated that no levy could be imposed upon shipping until the Lizard light was lit. But even then an official notification by Trinity House was required, which stated the light was fully operational. Until this document was received by the Lords of the Privy Council for Trade, Thomas Fonnereau had to bear the cost of the venture. [7]

Specifications of the Lizard Lighthouses

Trinity House appointed two Elder Brothers, Captain Joseph Cartert and Captain Edward Smith, to oversee the construction of the Lizard Point lighthouses. Although neither of them had any formal qualifications in building practises, they were experienced Master Mariners and well versed in the needs of shipping. It was their duty to ensure that the towers were positioned to provide the optimum visual aid for the mariner, both as day beacons and for the lights at night. Consideration was also given to the focal height of these lights and the illumination that was expected. Even the distance between the two towers was important, so that they were clearly distinguishable from each other when viewed from a ship on the horizon. [13]

An architect from Penzance was commissioned to draw up all of the plans, based upon the designs specified by the two Elder Brothers. However there are very few records which can give an insight to this architect.

By the time all of the drawings were prepared, the towers had been designated to be 216 ft (*65.84m*) apart. Each of the towers was to be built in an octagonal design, with its walls constructed from rubble granite masonry quarried from the headland.

At ground floor level the walls were 4 ft (*1.22m*) thick, which tapered externally to 2ft 9ins (*838mm*) at the course of masonry below its gallery. Access inside of the towers was by means of a geometrical stone stairway, which wound its way to the '*bellow blowers*' below the gallery. At this level a wooden pole ladder allowed the attendants to climb up to the lantern room. [13]

The actual lantern was constructed from cast iron framing with flat panes of glass. Its roof originally consisted of iron rafters covered with copper panels. On top of this conical roof was erected a large cylindrical chimney with a strange looking ball finial cowl.

Inside of each of the lanterns were large iron braziers. From below these units were iron pipes which fed air into the bottom portion of the coal fires. At the other ends of this network of pipes was large leather bellows. From some contemporary drawings it is assumed these bellows had step on and off planks of wood attached to them. Apparently it took two men to keep these bellows operational through the night. However to ensure the attendants never slacked in their duties, or went to sleep on the job, a watchman was employed. From his small cottage positioned between the two towers, he could see if the flame died down from lack of air or coal. If the light did not maintain its expected

Drawing of Lizard Point by Daniel Asher Alexander (1768-1846. Kind permission of Trinity House.

illumination, he would sound off a blow horn or fire a blast through his blunder bust which was primed with gun powder and dried corn. It is therefore not surprising that the records for the number of bellow blowers employed during this period was extremely high, when considering the men had to work from sunset to sunrise each night. [11]

Coal for the fires was either carried up the staircase, or hauled through the centre of the towers to the top of the lighthouse. On the floor below the bellow blowers area, was stored just enough coal for each nights requirements, with the remainder in an enclosure close to each tower. All of the cinders and ash was dumped inside of a rubble stoned walled trough, close to the watchman's cottage.

Thomas Fonnereau and his Cornish builders began the construction of the Lizard Point lighthouses on the 24th May 1750. On the night of the 15th July 1751 the two lights were officially lit for the first time. This event marked 127 years after Sir John Killigrew abandoned the original Lizard Point light. [13]

Extra Clauses Disputed in Lease

It was not until September 1752 that Thomas Fonnereau received his official lease documents for the Lizard lights. This delay was caused by one of the Corporation's surveyors who refused to sign the completion papers. This document verified that the station had been built according to the specifications laid down by Trinity House. During this period all of the financial burden for the construction programme and the cost of maintaining the coal fired lights for twelve months, had been paid for by Thomas Fonnereau. Yet he was not allowed to back date the loss of revenue due from the ships which had already passed the light. In reality this would have produced an income of £300 for that period, which was based upon the actual number of vessels recorded by the various attendants.

When reading through his lease papers Thomas Fonnereau was shocked to note two extra clauses added to the documents. One item stated that the rent would be reduced if the light was extinguished at a time of war, although he was led to believe he would be charged nothing if this situation arose. The main item which incensed him was the last clause which read: *'and after the expiry of the said period of 61 years, the lessee shall give up the lighthouses, buildings, roads ect., and one and a quarter acres of land known as Lizard Point, and to leave peaceably without a penny claim of compensation from the Corporation of Trinity House.'* [5]

He also felt insulted after being told his rent would not be reduced due to the extra cost involved in building the station. Originally he was led to believe that the Corporation would in fact make a certain concession with regards to this matter, especially as the completed project had cost double the original estimate. [11]

High Court Ruling

For 19 years Thomas Fonnereau battled with Trinity House, in an attempt to have the expiry clause deleted from his lease. His lawyers argued that the Corporation did not have the exclusive right to take over the land and property owned by their client. The Corporation stated that its Letter Patent clearly acknowledged that the Lizard light was classed as being in '*perpetuity*' and that unless a new lease was negotiated on the expiry of the existing one, it had the right to retain the land on which these important lights stood. But the lawyers still maintained that the Corporation had to pay compensation to Thomas Fonnereau or his descendants, for the privilege of taking over his land and property. In 1765 Thomas Fonnereau was forced to appeal against a judgement made in the High Court, which ruled that the original lease documents were legally binding.

For a further six years lawyers for both parties continued to drag the dispute through numerous courts of appeal, until in 1771 a panel of three judges and a jury decided the final outcome. It was felt by those concerned, that when considering the vast profits which were possible from the light dues over the 61 year period, the clauses were legal. They also stated that the contents of the original lease documents had been '*freely accepted*' by Thomas Fonnereau prior to the lighthouses being erected. In reality the only agreement for the lights, was base upon a '*Gentleman's Understanding*'. Legal fees for his unsuccessful court actions, plus the actual levy barely covering the cost of maintaining the lights, forced Thomas Fonnereau to declare himself bankrupt in 1780. [5]

At the beginning of 1781 Trinity House tried to find another lessee, after it had officially taken over the Lizard Point lights. For twelve months various offers were made, but each of them was subsequently withdrawn. On the 21st December 1781 the Corporation placed an advert in all of the local newspapers, which included the Exeter Flying Post and several National journals. It read: '*To be sold by Auction: Lease of Lizard Light Houses, 32 years unexpired: From Trinity House Corporation: Income very considerable: Paid Quarterly in London.*' However no one took up the option. Following this set back Trinity House decided to take over the full management of the lights and employ its own keepers to maintain them. [4]&[11]

Act of Parliament Required for Oil Lamps.

Coal remained the only authorised fuel source for the Lizard Point lights, until Trinity House issued a 'Notice to the Mariner' in the Royal Cornwall Gazette on the 29th December 1811. This followed two years of applications to Parliament to have the terms of the Letter Patent amended from coal to oil. Up to this time coal was considered a vital part of the economy, especially as every industry utilised this natural resource. Under the wording of the Patent lighthouses owners were forbidden to use any other form of fuel, unless an Act of Parliament was passed to change this important clause.

With the Act passed the notification to the mariner was issued. It read: '*Notice is hereby given, that this Corporation has, in compliance with the earnest and repeated requests of the Owners and Masters of Ships trading in and passing up and down the British Channel, directed the TWO LIGHTS at the LIZARD POINT, which have hitherto been shewn by Coal Fires, and found defective and generally complained of, to be altered to OIL LIGHTS; and necessary LANTHORNS and APPARATUS for the Purpose, are now erecting on the towers, and are expected to be completed on or about the 16th of January next; with Argand Lamps and Reflectors producing Lights of Great Brilliancy, that will be visible to a great distance in every direction, where requisite for the guidance of Navigation. Further notice will be given when alteration is completed and the improved Oil Lamps exhibited.'* [5]

On the 11th January 1812 the promised notification was published in the Royal Cornwall Gazette and by the following Thursday, the 16th January, the new lights were lit for the first time.

The work carried out to complete this project entailed the erection of two trellis style timber towers beside each of the existing lighthouses. However the illumination from the three enclosed Argand lamps and catoptric reflectors, installed in both of the temporary lanterns, was extremely low. On numerous occasions sailing vessels ran dangerously close to the treacherous coastline before the lights became visible.

Dismantling of the old lanterns and the removal of the battered remains of the former coal braziers, brought cheers from the over worked bellow blowers. There was a small item in the Royal Cornwall Gazette, which featured some comments from these attendants. They stated that it was time to go back to fishing or into the mines, but this would be less arduous and back breaking job when compared to the all night pumping of the bellows. [4]

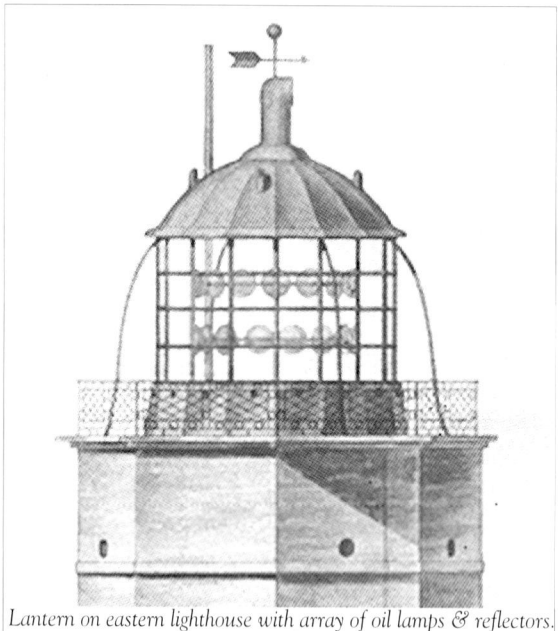

The new lanterns were made locally in an iron foundry near Penzance, then transported in a kit form to Lizard Point. When erected on top of the towers these conical roofed lanterns stood nearly 13ft (*3.96m*) in height and just over 10ft (*3m*) in diameter. The actual towers had been increased in height to about 61ft (*18.6m*) from the ground floor level to the top of the wind vane surmounted on the lantern.

Lantern on eastern lighthouse with array of oil lamps & reflectors. Kind permission of Trinity House.

Both lanterns consisted of a cast iron pedestal base, on to which was erected an 8ft (*2.44m*) high glazed framing. This section was formed out of cast iron glazing bars with numerous flat panes of glass. On top was formed a conical roof with a large copper chimney. However any thoughts for ventilating the lantern had been forgotten, which saw numerous holes being drilled through the sides of the pedestal base. Inside the lantern was erected an iron column on to which was fixed 19 Argand lamps, each with its own 21in (*533mm*) in diameter and 9in (*229mm*) deep catoptric reflector. All of these reflectors were made of polished silvered copper and considered to be the most expensive items fitted during this modernisation programme. [13]

When these new fixed position lights were brought into service on Thursday 16th January 1812, they had a recorded visible distance on a clear night of nearly 21 nautical miles. However many Masters on board passing ships, stated that at times the glow of the Lizard Point lights could be seen from well below the horizon. [1]

Not During Divine Worship

About half way through the modernisation programme, various problems arose. Late delivery of materials, lack of suitable labour and very extreme weather conditions, seriously delayed the project. To overcome these difficulties the Corporation instructed its consultant engineer, Daniel Asher Alexander, to keep the workers employed seven days a week. However this directive brought condemnation from the local Church Elders, who threatened to take the Corporation to court. Their complaint was the fact that the men were working on a Sunday, which was the Lord's Day. This action was considered to be sacrilegious, but Trinity House ignored the threat and forced the matter in front of the Penzance Magistrates. [4]

• For nearly three days the lawyers for both sides gave their points of view. When the Magistrates deliberated on the facts, the Church Elders were told to withdraw their action. These wise old Magistrates had made a very diplomatic ruling, which stated that the need for the lights was a '*dire necessity for humanitarian reasons.*' This being for the preservation of the mariner. However they did stipulate that the men were not allowed to work '*during divine worship*', which was to be signalled by the sounding of the church bells. The local Parish Church had three services each Sunday, which effectively halved the number of hours the men could work. [5]

Family Status Quarters

Once the new lights were operational the second phase of the modernisation programme commenced. This work entailed the demolition of the night watchman's cottage and the construction of a 216ft (*65.8m*) long building between the two towers.

When viewed at ground level this building appeared to be a single storey structure, but provision was made for a basement workshop, oil store and wash house. Water storage tanks were sunk in strategic positions to the rear of the building and cast iron manually operated lift pumps installed on top.

Accommodation was also required for the expected eight keepers and their families who would be living on station. When the first of these keepers were posted to Lizard Point, the number of people literally turned the station into a mini village. Originally the complement of personnel and their families amounted to thirty six men, women and children. However this also swelled by the number of farm yard animals which provided nearly all of the stations food stuffs.

In 1814 the final accounts for modernising Lizard Point, were presented to the Privy Council for Trade by Trinity House. The cost of the project had amounted to £10,278. If comparison is made at today's prices, this figure would be around £750,000. [19]

****

Cherubim & Ocean Home

Progression to steam saw ships covering much straighter and faster courses at sea. This in turn necessitated the need for navigation lights to be visible from greater distances. Timing for these lights was normally based upon a steam vessel travelling about twenty miles in two hours. With ships under sail and traversing on a zig zag pattern, this same distance could take between four or five hours. With the new Lizard Point lights providing a positive reference for fixing a ships position, the number of vessels being wrecked along this stretch of Cornish coast was greatly reduced. Yet vessels still fell foul of the dangerous waters around the headland. Also these were the early days before the protocol for steam ships to give way to those under sail became the rule of the mariner. This situation is believed to be the cause of a tragic collision close to Lizard Point.

On the 5th September 1856 the 646 ton American sailing ship *Ocean Home*, approached Lizard Point enroute to New York from Rotterdam. Her Master altered course to a heading which he believed would steer his passenger ship clear of Land's End. But as she passed the Lizard lights the American steamer *Cherubim*, bound for the north east of England, rammed the *Ocean Home* amidships.

Sailing ship similar to Ocean Home. Acknowledgment J.C. Medland

The speed of this collision allowed no time for any of the lifeboats on the *Ocean Home* to be lowered before she sank. Off duty lighthouse keepers, Coast Guard officers and numerous local people, tried in vain to get ropes to the frantic people attempting to swim ashore. But the bitterly cold heavy seas took a tragic toll on these people, many drowning because of the weight of their sodden clothing. To the helpless people gathered on the shoreline, all they could do was to watch this gruesome scene unfolding in front of them.

Although seriously damaged and taking on a lot of water through the bow compartment, the Master of the *Cherubim* and his crew threw life rafts and lines to the stricken people bobbing in the sea. Sadly the atrocious conditions saw the loss of four crew men, who launched one of the steamer's lifeboats in a brave attempt at rescuing the drowning people. As the boat was being lowered over the side of the ship a huge wave smashed it to pieces, throwing the helpless men into the sea. Their bodies were never found.

The sad remnants of the people from the *Ocean Home*, were dragged out of the sea and taken on board the *Cherubim*. After more than an hour her Master reluctantly ordered his crew to give up the search. His only concern was the increasing volume of water forcing its way into the steamer. The pumps were barely keeping up with the tremendous flow, so it was imperative that the *Cherubim* reached Falmouth as quickly as possible.

Local Coast Guard officers reported at the Board of Trade Inquiry, that there seemed to be no reason for the collision. From their vantage point near the lighthouse, it appeared that neither ship took any action to prevent the tragic incident. From a complement of 105 passengers and crew on board the *Ocean Home only* 28 survived. Her Captain was also lost along with his wife and three children. [2] & [8]

Lizard Lifeboat and the Czar

To many people it will seem strange that a Lifeboat service was not established near Lizard Point until 1859. This was a tragic situation when considering the disastrous record of ships being wrecked along these shores, made the area the worse around the whole of England.

However the events which finally led up to the introduction of the Lizard Lifeboat service happened on the 22nd January 1859. This tragic incident involved the iron steam ship *Czar*, which was wrecked after running into the submerged Vogue Rock. Her complement consisted of Captain Robert Jackson, his wife and small children, plus eighteen crew. This tragic incident happened so quickly that the *Czar* broke in two and sank within twenty minutes with only eight men surviving.

When a prominent Cornish landowner, T.J.Agar Roberts, heard about the tragedy and the heroic actions of the Coast Guard officers, lighthouse keepers and local people who carried out the rescue in small rowing boats, he decided it was time that something more positive was done to remedy the situation. [3]

After reading through the report about the loss of the *Czar*, he instructed his land agent Alfred Jenkins to send a letter to the Lifeboat Institution Headquarters, with an offer to purchase a boat for Lizard Point. By the end of April 1859 a reply was received from Captain Ward R.N. (*retired*), the Inspector for the Lifeboat Institution, thanking Mr. Roberts for his generous offer. However this promised donation not only allowed for the provision of a purpose built vessel, but the cost of purchasing a boat house and finance for the construction work and labour.

Land owned by Agar Roberts at Polpeor was to be the site for the Lifeboat house and launching stage. This offer was formerly accepted and by November 1859, the 30ft (*9.14m*) long, six oared, self righting *Anna Maria*, arrived in Falmouth. The naming of the Lifeboat was dedicated to Agar Roberts mother.

The arrival of the Lifeboat took a route along the main road to Falmouth on the 8th November, which brought out hundreds of people who crowded the streets trying to catch a glimpse of this wonderful boat.

The total cost for this Lifeboat project, included £135 for the *Anna Maria*, £119 for the boat house and its launch staging, £15 for the carriage charges, with Agar Roberts donating a full kit (*including life jackets*) for all of the volunteer crewmen. Its record of rescues makes fascinating reading. [18]

31

Discovery of Sir Michael Faraday

Electricity was introduced to the Lizard Point lights in 1878. It was described by A.G.Finlay in his 1885 List of Lighthouses as: '*the most wonderful means now employed in lighthouses, whether it is viewed as the result of the most exalted science or of the consummate skill which utilises this mysterious agent. Naturally this very complicated question resolves itself in two portions. The means employed to produce the power and the apparatus required for utilising it.*' These were clearly the problems which arose with the modernisation to electrical operation at Lizard Point. [14]

Yet it must be mentioned that in 1837, forty seven years before electricity was introduced any where in the World, Michael Faraday (*later to be Knighted for his achievements in science*) had discovered this '*strange and mysterious*' power source. He wound insulated copper wire around a cylindrical magnet. Then by moving the magnet backwards and forward inside of this coil of wire electricity was produced. Yet Faraday's discovery was first considered by the recognised scientific body as a '*novelty*'. For nearly twenty years no further development or formal research was carried out with this new power source. [15] & [9]

However with Michael Faraday in his position of the Scientific Officer for Trinity House, was able to convince its Committee to allows numerous experiments to be carried out at the Dungeness and South Foreland lighthouse stations. But to produce enough electricity during these early times required enormous steam engines coupled to massive dynamo generation sets.

In 1874 Trinity House posted its '*Notice to Mariners*' in the Cornish Telegraph and numerous national newspapers, about the intention of converting the Lizard Point lights to electrical operation. [17]

Near the end of November 1874 James Nicholas Douglass, the Corporations Engineer-in-Chief, supervised the start of the modernisation programme. His designs for the Lizard station included the construction of a large engine room, a coal and coke store, a full size workshop and a purpose built engineers apartment. There was also quarters built for the expected

Sir Michael Faraday (1791-1867)

four keepers who would be required to maintain the new equipment and machinery. To ensure suitable accommodation was provided, the designs specified that the existing roof on the centralised dwellings should be removed and a second storey constructed on top of the existing building. [15]

Inside of the spacious machine room were installed three 10 h.p. (*horse power*) calorific engines, all to be fuelled by either anthracite coal or coke. The reason for using this expensive high quality coal, was because it contained more than 85% carbon and burnt with a much cleaner flame. Its composition also ensured it contained the minimal amount of volatile material (*such as pockets of compressed gases*), which could explode and cause various problems with the engines. The units installed at Lizard Point at this time, were engines manufactured by A & F Brown of New York. Their working speed provided 60 r.p.m. of drive power. When in service two of the engines ran simultaneously. These units were set up to drive four large generators by means of webbed belts gripping huge cast iron wheels fixed to a long steel shaft. The third engine was for the sole use of driving the air compressor that powered the fog siren. [15]

Each of the large Holmes dynamo electric generators was capable of producing enough power for the carbon arc lamps to provide a mean intensity of nearly 3,320 candle power (*candelas*). It was the normal practise for only one engine to be in service to drive two of the generators, with the other unit kept on 'trickle burn' as a standby. Also the standard operational method was to ensure the engines received equal wear and tear and every weekend one of them was taken out of service with the third brought in. During heavy

33

Brown Brothers Caloric engines prior to the modernisation programme of 1903. A special acknowledgment to Trinity House for the use of this irreplaceable pictures.

mist, fog or snow, all of the generators would be in use. Their combined employment produced a energy source of approximately 8,250 candle power (*candelas*). [15]

However when comparing today's safety standards for electricity, at Lizard Point the original d.c. power cables were thick wires of 90% grade copper coated in rubber. It was necessary to provide as much air circulation as possible around these wires to prevent them from over heating and catching fire. To achieve this the cables were hung from straps and elongated clips fixed to timber back boards. During several experiments at Dungeness it was noted that a large quantity of the rubber bubbled, especially for the cables clipped to the walls. [17]

The carbon arc lamps were designed by Dr. John Hopkinsson (F.R.S.), with three of these pieces of equipment installed in each of the optical apparatus. Yet only two of these lamps would be in operation at the same time with the third set up on standby. Chance Brothers of Smethick, Birmingham, manufactured these lamps, with the carbon rods produced and supplied by Seimens. The design of these lamps had a simple weight which dropped according to a small clockwork mechanism. This system was intended to ensure the burning ends of the carbon rods remained at their optimum distance to produce the brightest light and to stay in operation. In theory this worked, but the calculations only allowed for clear weather operation. During heavy weather when the power level was increased, the rods burnt away much faster. Without being able to adjust the rate of turns correctly on the clock, the keepers had to revert back to the former Douglass multi-wick

The noise inside of the Lizard Point engine room around 1903 must have been tremendous. A special acknowledgment to Trinity House.

burners. [15]

Brightest Lights Around England & Powerful Fog Siren

While the changes to electricity were in progress, the engineers from Chance Brothers installed a first order dioptric lens assembly into each of the lantern rooms. Both of these units was capable of magnifying the light source to a phenomenal 8 million candle power (*candelas*). The recorded visible distance for these lights was reputed to be about 22 nautical miles. This was the considered intensity required by the mariner on board a steam ship.

The new lights caused a great deal of media interest. The Cornish Telegraph reported that hundreds of people came to see this *'Amazing Phenomenon'*, when they were first lit on the 29th March 1878. However the lights had one particular problem and that was the expensive carbon rods. The expected life span of these items failed to live up to the manufacturers specifications. This forced Trinity House to instruct its keepers to revert back to the oil burners until the matter was resolved.

When the modernisation work was in progress, James Nicholas Douglass visited Lizard Point to see the new fog siren. Based upon the original Patented designs of A & F Brown of New York, this engineer had adapted this unit so that it operated with compressed air instead of the intended steam pressure.

Author informed that this is the last remaining picture of the Douglass fog siren in full working order. Possible telescope can be seen on siren casing. Special acknowledgment to Trinity House.

    The Douglass unit consisted of a hollow brass drum 6ins (*150mm*) in diameter and 9½ins (*236mm*) long. Formed along its length were twelve slits about 8ins (*205mm*) long by ½in (*12.5mm*) wide. Inside of this cylindrical unit was a smaller tube with similar perforations. When compressed air was forced through the inner cylinder revolved at 2,400 r.p.m. The powerful sound produced was then transmitted out of 15ft (*4.57m*) long cast iron trumpets which had 18in (*457mm*) tapered bell mouths. These upright hooked shaped trumpets were designed so that the keepers could rotate them in any direction on top of the fog signal house. This was to ensure that they sounded off in the optimum position according to the prevailing wind direction. [15]

    On the 20th January 1878 Trinity House published its notification in the Cornish Telegraph and other National newspapers, which informed the readers that the Lizard Point fog siren would be tested the following day. However not everyone in the locality bought the London Times or the Cornish Telegraph. The result caused quite an uproar, with many of the people in the close vicinity not happy about the noise produced. A report on this event was published in the Cornish Telegraph on the 22nd January. It read: ' *To those, however, in close proximity, it must be very annoying and by night sleep disturbing. It was blown from 4 a.m. to 8 a.m. yesterday morning. There it rolls, with long reverberating echoes sounding through the surrounding precipices and caves*'.

Majestic fog horns dated around 1950. Original chimney stacks still in position. Kind permission of Trinity House.

When the final accounts were presented to Trinity House and to the Institution of Civil Engineers in 1879, by James Nicholas Douglass, the breakdown read as follows:

Buildings & Lanterns   £7,636
Dynamo electric machinery & optics   £5,500
For the works, exclusive of fog signal   £13,136
Add cost of fog signal   £1,806

Making total of   £28,072

For this period of time in lighthouse history, the cost of modernising the Lizard Point lights was a very *'Princely'* sum. [15]

Loss of the Suffolk

Even with the introduction of one of the most powerful sirens around England, fog remained one of the mariner's major nightmares near Lizard Point. On the 28th September 1886 the three mast schooner rigged steamship, *Suffolk*, ploughed bow first into Old Lizard Head. The impact crumpled her mid section and within a few hours the sea broke her in two. [10]

Lifeboats from Cadgwith and Lizard rescued all of her forty passengers and crew. However, only 26 out of 161 cattle on board survived. Many of the local people tried to pacify the frantic animals, but they stampeded and jumped into the sea.

Only One Light

The advances in electrical equipment and more efficient machinery, soon made the original Holmes generators obsolete. These giant permanent magnet alternator units had clearly provided the Lizard lights with all of the necessary power. But the running cost and maintenance for the Brown Brothers engines was not economically viable. During the summer months of 1895 the first two diesel oil engines were installed. Only one of the former calorific engines was retained and today it has been preserved as a tourist attraction. [1]

Suffolk breaking in two just before sinking. Acknowledgment to Richard Larn.

By this time sail had given away to the more reliable and cost effective steam ships, which could cover much faster and straighter courses. Observation of the Lizard Point station had proved that the need for two lights was not necessary. Ship owners and Masters requested Trinity House to considered exhibiting just one light and to upgrade the equipment to a revolving and a distinctive flashing characteristic. By 1903 the Corporation had decided to discontinue the west light and install a new optical apparatus and clockwork drive mechanism into the eastern tower.

On the 1st November 1903 the new Chance Brothers revolving first order optic was brought in to service. Its intensity was recorded to be 12 million candle power (*candelas*), with the beam of light visible for 26 nautical miles. This figure was often disputed by the Masters of numerous ships, who stated that the Lizard light could be seen as a very distinct

Wonderful view from inside the Lizard Point optic and its lamp changer with filament bulbs. Kind permission of Trinity House.

glow from well below the horizon. During these changes a new method of light source was being experimented with and this was the vapour burner. Although not officially introduced until 1904, the Arthur Kitson invention was tested at Lizard Point and Blackwall during this period. [13]

A World at War (1914-18)

During the early part of the First World War Lizard Point became a prime observation post for the British Admiralty. Yet even with this new status no harm ever came to the lighthouse. Numerous German submarines were spotted close to the Cornish Coast, with one in particular running for the safety of Wolf Rock. Her Captain must have been extremely lucky, because he managed to position his U Boat right against the rocks. But at low tide the submarine became stranded. Information about this vessel originally came from the keepers, although at the time these men believed they were simply noting the movement of shipping. [2] & [10]

Like many of the lights around the South coast of England, Lizard Point could only be lit on the orders of the Admiralty and then just at half power. The purpose of this was to assist the passing of Allied convoys heading to the north east of England. Yet the elusive U Boats played havoc with these undefended coal carrying coasters, which sailed slowly around Land's End. Observations from Lizard Point saw numerous ships exploding after being

The fated Bardic. Acknowledgment to Richard Larn.

torpedoed. Even though they were putting their own lives at risk, the volunteer Lifeboat men from both Cadgwith and Lizard rescued hundreds of mariners during this four year hostile period. Communication was one of the main obstacles for the keepers, whose only means of signalling at this time was either flags or flashing hand held lamps. The telegraph system did not come to Lizard Point until 1920, when Marconi completed his experiments in the purpose built shack on Bass Point. This building is still there and is being preserved by the Trevithick Trust.

Refrigerator Ship Bardic

During thick fog in late August 1924 the *Bardic* was almost run down by an Atlantic passenger liner as she drifted towards the Lizard reef. But this sturdy vessel was later refloated and repaired. After being sold she was renamed on several occasions until she was one of the unlucky ships to be shelled by the German battleship Scharnhorst in 1941. [3]

A New Light Source

In 1926 Lizard Point was one of the first lighthouses in the British Isles to have the new Edison filament bulbs fitted. Experiments carried out in America proved that his method of electric light was more economical, safer and lasted much longer than the existing carbon arc rods. Although very large in size these new bulbs were no more difficult to change than unscrewing the top of a bottle. It was mentioned that the keepers would not have any problem in carrying out this small task, as this was something they were well versed in doing.

Over the next few years further bulbs and lamps were tested at Lizard Point, with man of the electrical assemblies manufactured by Chance Brothers. By this time the company was diversifying its interests into other fields of technology, apart from its recognised major international share of designing and manufacturing of lanterns and optical

Mercury vapour bulb known for its green light. Trinity House.

40

assemblies.

By the start of the Second World War Lizard Point was still considered to have the brightest light around the coast of England, even though its intensity was greatly reduced to just 5.25 million candle power (*candelas*).

An Air Borne War

In 1939 the Second World War brought a different form of attack and this was from the air. The keepers at Lizard Point witnessed the havoc of numerous raids by the Luftwaffe as these planes bombed ships anchored in Falmouth harbour. The night time sky use to light up as each explosion found a target, yet the lighthouse remained virtually untouched. However on several occasions the tower was used for target practise by the gunners in these planes, but most of the aggression was aimed at the local radar station.

As with most lighthouse stations, so called camouflage experts blacked out Lizard Point. Numerous shutters and panels were used to cover the windows. But one ingenious keeper decided to make good use of some of these old shutters and built a splendid grand father clock. It is still in full working order, which is due to the care and dedication of its maker Keeper John Ellis.

John Ellis timepiece. Author's collection

'Tell them I'm polishing the lantern glass'

Communications for the keepers at Lizard Point continued with the Morse telegraph system. This applied to any ship to shore contact or to the regional depot at Penzance. But in 1940 things took a more positive step forward.

On the 5th February Lizard Point had its first telephone installed. Its

'No dear we don't put the cat out at night on the Needles.' Permission of Trinity House.

41

Former electrical control panel. Author's collection.

number was Lizard 231. Even today this is still the last three digits for calling the station. However it soon became apparent that Trinity House could contact the keepers at any time. But during the Second World War, this system became extremely important for reporting the movement of shipping. Yet in later years one of the favourite excuses for a keeper not being able to come to the phone was *'tell them I'm polishing the lantern glass'*.

Connection to National Power Grid

Seventy two years after electricity first came to the Lizard Point lighthouse, Trinity

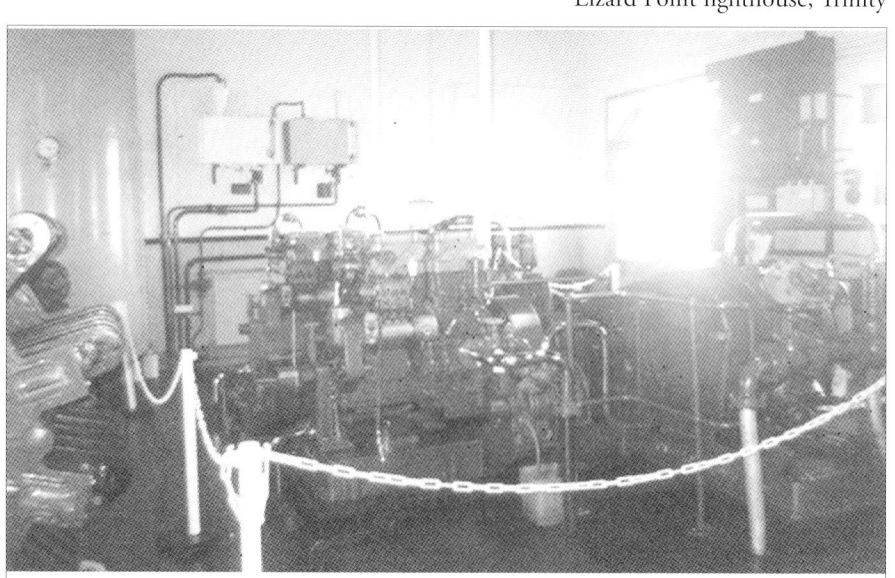

Lovingly preserved machinery at Lizard Point. Author's collection.

House finally managed to have the station connected to the National power supply. It had taken many years of negotiation to have a mains electric cable brought down to the lighthouse. This work also provided nearly everyone in the village with the opportunity to have electricity as well.

Two of the existing generators and diesel engines were upgraded to act a standby units in case of mains failure. However there was no automatic change over system at this time. If the power failed a clockwork bell would sound. At night the obvious sign was no lights, but during the daytime this was not always apparent. For the keepers, they had to start the generator engines by hand after ensuring the mains supply was isolated. To turn everything off the large lever on the black supply box fixed to the engine room wall had to be pushed upwards. Even today this takes a great deal of effort although this system is no longer in use but retained for show.

Treasured Holmes generator at Lizard Point. Author's collection.

The Lives of the Keepers

For 380 years the Lizard Point has in one way or another, been associated with a navigational light. Yet it is true to say that the life of a keeper only truly began in 1751. Attendants of the former Killigrew lighthouse did provide a light, but as history has already shown it was more often extinguished than lit.

Life for any lighthouse keeper through the years has grown to a sense of deep pride, to be a person in this traditional employment. To be a Mister Fix it, with a wonderful sense of humour and the ability to endure the confines of a rock based tower for up to three months at a time, was some of the main qualities Trinity House required. There also had to be a high degree of responsible attitude to the positions that they held, with honesty a very important item.

Sadly automation has taken away the need for the manual task, with these former dedicated people becoming redundant from something that was more than a job but a way of life. Ask any former traditonal keeper if they would return to the service and the answer

Deputy Master Rear Admiral Rowe hides the Duke of Edinburgh from view during his speech at the handing over of North Foreland. P.K. Dermot Cronin (centre) and his fellow keepers are stood with the Operations Director Captain King. Author's collection.

would be yes.

One of the hardest things for the last of these keepers is coming to terms with the fact that they never achieved one special goal. This was the chance to retire after completing their full tour of duty. They also know that no one will ever become a lighthouse keeper in the true traditional way. So to be called the last keeper is something none of them wanted to be. Yet this honour was bestowed on Principal Keeper Dermot Cronin in November 1998, when he officially handed over the North Foreland station in Broadstairs, Kent, following its automation.

But there is a slight twist to this story which revolves around the charismatic personality of former Principal Keeper Michael J.Matthews, or Eddie to everyone who has ever met him. This unconventional Cornishman was due to have the sad honour of being the last P.K. for Trinity House, but he decided to remain at his post at the Lizard Point lighthouse as its attendant.

To give a brief insight to this genuine and down to earth, yet extremely proud Cornishman, it is important to take a look at his life as a keeper. He firstly flaunted the rules

'Do you known mate, Trinity House has just given me a load of 8ft (2.44m) high posters to put around the station. God knows who'll be doing this job.' Forever Eddie Matthews. Author's collection.

of the Corporation by fibbing about his age. The rule was that he had to be eighteen before joining the service, but at the interview he was only seventeen and a half. '*Well, what's six months among friends,*' is Eddie's comment. So in 1958 Michael J.Matthews was accepted for the post of supernumerary keeper.

At this time he had no idea that his first posting was to be the same lighthouse at which he would end his career as its Principal Keeper. Nor did he realise he would become the star of radio and television.

His life has been one of many enjoyments in a job which he has excelled in over the years. But his style of working has often brought comments from his superiors, because he bends the rules of dressing up in official clothes to times when he is ordered to do so. Yet at no time is there any element of disrespect towards the Corporation of Trinity House.

His first Principal Keeper who took him under his wing in 1958 was Gordon Stevens, a man who Eddie had a great deal of respect for. He initially went to Harwich where instruction was given as to the way he should present himself as a keeper and how to cook a loaf of bread by the ever cheerful Tex Ritter. Among many other things one of his main duties was to be very conversant with the Hood burners, which at times could be very temperamental.

Eddie has been posted to numerous lighthouses, with Lundy Island holding special memories. On one occasion at the local inn, a new keeper walked into the bar in civilian clothes. Mrs Gates, the landlady, introduced herself and welcomed the new keeper. Eddie was rather surprised as no one had told her about this new addition to the team. So he asked her how she knew he was a keeper. The reply was *'the smell'*. Eddie then wanted to know what she meant, to which he was told about the '*piddle and paraffin.*' Without a doubt Eddie knew exactly what she was talking about. The smell of mineral oil impregnated every piece of clothing, no matter what the keepers did to prevent it. Also if they were not careful with the '*bucket and chuck it*', the wind blew the spray from the contents of the can back over their clothes.

The Hood burner. Trinity House.

He has never been one to follow convention in any way. He believes that you should be able to enjoy yourself, but make sure you do your job properly as well. This was very apparent on a hot summers day whilst stationed at Lynmouth Foreland. With all of the duties completed Eddie and two of his companions decided to go to an inn near Pollock Hill. At the lighthouse they left a supernumerary to keep an eye on things. However they did tell the young keeper where they were going in case he needed them. There was one problem and that was the transport being used. This old Ford Prefect had no tax and was a bit of a wreck, but the three keepers decided to take the chance for a bit of refreshment. Just in case the police were around they left their transport in a car park a short distance up the hill then walked down to the inn. Five pints of ale later the phone rang and Eddie was informed that the superintendent was on his way to carry out an inspection.

Affectionately remembered. Lynmouth Foreland. Author's collection.

'But what about the photographer and the ship he was on when this tremendous picture was taken?'
Kind permission of Frank Gibson. May you soon take photos once more.

They all charged out of the inn and back to the car but the blasted thing would not start. While at the inn someone believed the car had been abandoned and took the battery. Panic set in as they tried to get one of the regulars to give them an '*emergency*' lift back to the lighthouse. With minutes to spare they were changed and ready for the inspection. But the superintendent wanted to know why one of them was so out of breath. To which the reply was '*just making sure everything was tidy.*' Yet there was this keeper all dressed up in his uniform as if he had just been for a final walk around the station, with the superintendent trying to understand why he was wearing brown suede shoes.

There is a very serious side to Eddie Matthews, apart from his love of football and this is the memories of life on the Wolf Rock. He remembers vividly the time when hurricane force weather conditions battered the station during the winter months of 1958-59. The conditions were so bad it was impossible for the keepers to be relieved for three months. At this time Eddie's companions were Principal Keeper Thomas (*Tommy*) Davis and Assistant keepers Howard Allen and William (*Bill*) Trevillcock.

Waves crashed into the tower as if it was literally trying to shake it from its foundations. The cacophony of noise inside this granite lighthouse was unbelievable. Every few seconds the sea would funnel its way up the side of the tower and crash against the gun metal storm shutters. Yet surprisingly the keepers remained calm and even managed to sleep through all of the upheaval.

When asked about things that had become treasured memories, Eddie stated it was when the emergency ration cupboard had to be opened due to not being relieved. It was like luxury when a tin of 50 Players Navy Cut cigarettes was first opened and the magic seal broken. The smell was terrific. He also delighted in opening the tins of corn beef, although there was never any need for the keepers to eat all 200 tins. Yet they did their best.

In the medicine cabinet was a special bottle of rum *'purely for medicinal purposes only of course'* about which he was asked who was responsible for keeping a check on its contents. His reply was *'nobody checked. Any way that is a trade secret'*.

It must be remembered that Eddie has experienced not only the forces of nature that pound into a rock based tower, but like so many other unsung keepers the delights of being dumped into the sea during a relief.

Boatman George Hicks who along with generations of his family covered the keepers relief for Bishop Rock. F. Gibson

As the years have gone by you might think that Eddie would have mellowed with age. But even after 42 years as a keeper he still retains that unique outlook on life. To him there is still a lot to do and many things to see, yet he will always do it in his own style. These days his favourite outfit is a donkey jacket, open necked shirt, a well worn pair of trousers and his special soft brown shoes. To finish off this keepers uniform he adorns his head, not with the traditional peaked service hat, but a base ball cap. To ensure he never loses touch with anyone, he also carries around his white mobile phone. Who calls him nobody knows, but he is already for anyone who does.

In style he joined the service and through his career he has maintained this wonderful personality. This is apparent when looking through the station order book. *'Station inspected and found to be in excellent order. Moral at lighthouse of the highest calibre, which is commendable to Principal Keeper Matthews.*'

Now living on station as the resident attendant keeper, Eddie Matthews continues to lovingly care for the lighthouse where he has lived for the past ten years. Visitors can be assured of a wonderful welcome, with far more stories than could ever be put into this publication. There will often be the smell of freshly cut grass, as Eddie still makes sure the grounds are in pristine conditions. If asked he will show you the cheekiest rabbits in Cornwall, which will actually pose for photos.

'What do you expect? The wife's got the car.'
Author's collection.

The Final Days Automation

It seems that all of our lives revolve around acts of war, although most of us do not comprehend how. In fact technology which was originally devised for surveillance, has now been redeployed for the betterment of saving lives.

When a satellite went into orbit a means of controlling its operation was devised using high frequency radio waves. Known as the telemetry system, it allowed precise monitoring from a land based control centre thousands of miles away. Today most of us take this technology very much for granted, as we sit in our comfortable chairs and press buttons on plastic hand sets to change the television programmes.

This system was the first sign of the automation and de-manning programme for lighthouses around the coasts of the

St. Anthonys lighthouse

49

British Isles. Firstly many of the land based stations were set up to be controlled and monitored by the major first order establishments. Then helipads were erected on top of the rock based towers, which not only made the keepers relief a certainty, but also allowed new equipment and machinery to be brought out to these lighthouses.

In a relatively short space of time the death bell tolled for the keepers, until one by one the rock based stations were automated. On the 18th January 1989 Lizard Point became the south west monitoring station, for Longships, Wolf Rock, Round Island, St. Anthony's and the Seven Stones light vessel. The keepers at Lizard Point then carried out routine maintenance as attendants for these stations, on top of their normal duties.

Round Island two weeks before the keepers left. Permission of Trinity House.

On the 17th March 1989 the Lizard Point light was provided with new high efficiency 400 watt lamp which greatly increased its intensity. Yet when compared to the former lamps, it was not any bigger than a standard household bulb.

Also at this time the existing 'N' signal diaphone, which sounded off every 60 seconds, was removed and replaced by a new fog emitter that provided a 3 second blast every 30 seconds. On the gallery was fixed an automatic atmospheric sensor, which brought the fog warning signal into operation.

Time continued to roll on by with the final tour of duty looming ever closer for the keepers at Lizard Point. But they were not forgotten by

Longships before its heli-pad. Kind permission of Trinity House.

The Sevenstones light vessel shortly before its crew covered their last tour of duty. Kind permission of Trinity House.

the Association of Lighthouse Keepers (ALK) a special organisation established in 1988. This Society was formed by past and present time served keepers, with the aim of remaining in contact with everyone after the redundancies. Yet this idea has escalated to where enthusiasts from all over the World are now joining this very special association. So with this in mind the dedicated founder members of this society, namely Grahame Fearn, Neil Hargreaves and Peter Williams, provided the keepers at the last remaining manned lighthouses a final Christmas hamper.

In conjunction with Tesco's supermarkets, these gifts were presented just before Christmas 1997. At Penzance a man over heard a member of the Tesco staff mention that the hamper was for the keepers at Lizard Point. To everyone's amazement this man handed over his credit card and asked the staff to do a two minute

DGPS mast to east of Lizard Point. Author's collection.

51

*Scaffolding during automation work.
Lizard Point lantern with the new items.*

supermarket trolley dash. Once the goods were at the check out the man calmly signed his docket and left the store. He never gave his name, nor waited to be thanked. All he said was " *if its for the lighthouse keepers; well they deserve it.*" Maybe someone who reads this item might know who this unsung hero was?

This particular hamper was presented to Eddie Matthews and his fellow keepers, which came as a very pleasant surprise. Similar had overs of hampers occurred almost simultaneously at St. Ann's (*to Phil Griffiths and his companions*) at Nash Point (*to Dermot Cronin and his companions*) and at North Foreland (*to Gerry Douglass Sherwood and his companions*), being the last of the four manned stations.

In less than six months, on the 15th April 1998, Trinity House engineers arrived at Lizard Point to install the new satellite navigation system (*DGPS*) along with its tall mast. It was also a sad day for the keepers who had just completed their last tour of duty.

Three months later the '*LAST*' keepers returned proudly wearing their service uniforms, to officially hand over the lighthouses station following its automation. In the station order book, or journal, is the following entry:

'*16th July 1998 The Deputy Master Rear Admiral P.B.Rowe CBE LVO, accompanied by the Director of Operations Captain P.H.King, Director of Engineering Malcolm Wannell, attended the ceremony to mark post-automation and demanning of Lizard Point lighthouse, after 247 years of keepership. Last Keepers: Michael Matthews P.K. John Turney A.K. David Spurgeon A.K.*'

Today all aspects of the operational side of Lizard Point is monitored from the Trinity House control centre in Harwich.

Because the bulbs hang from the rafters.

Why the empty bulb and lamp cabinet?

Like other stories associated with lighthouses, some tend to exaggerate the historical facts about the local communities. Around Cornwall it has been well documented about the activities of wreckers, pirates and smugglers, but how much of it is really true can only be assumed. The only factual statement that can be made about this historical light station, is that its existence has helped to save the lives of thousands of mariners who have sailed up and down the English Channel.

Its light has guided countless ships passed the deadly coast of Cornwall. It was once written that *'lighthouses do not prevent ship wrecks, they only give the mariner the means to avoid the dangers that they mark.'* Without a doubt Lizard Point has provided this very special service.

But this story would not be complete without telling you about what has been left out of this publication. There are many wonderful pieces of equipment being preserved as part of our heritage, which former keepers such as Eddie Matthews religiously protect. This is possible with the Trevithick Trust which has taken on the task of Lizard Point within its role of preserving the heritage of Cornwall. Trinity House plays a major role with this lighthouse, so between these two enterprises this *'Grand Old Lady'* still shines. However visitors need to call to keep this station alive.

Ships in bulbs by P.K. Ivor Prichard (retired)

Reference Sources

1. *Report of the Commissioners for Buoys, Beacons & Lights (2793) XXV (1861)*
2. *The Sea Thine Enemy* by Captain Kenneth Langmaid DSC. RN. Published by Jarrolds Publishers (LONDON) (1966)
3. *Cornish Shipwrecks (South Coast)* by Clive Carter & Richard Larn. Published by David & Charles, Newton Abbott, Devon. (1969)
4. *Cornish Studies Library, Redruth Cornwall.*
5. *Truro Record Office.*
6. *Trinity House Minute Book Guildhall Library (1624)*
7. *The Statutes at Large from Magna Carta to the Union of the Kingdoms of Great Britain and Ireland.* Edited by John Raithley (20 vols.) London (1811)
8. *Records from the Hydrograhic Office for the Ministry of Defence Taunton, Somerset, England. (1600-1995) Extensive files.*
9. *Diaries of George Burrell - National Library of Wales (1835-1842)*
10. *Cornish Lights and Shipwrecks* by Cyril Noall. Published by D. Bradford Barton Ltd. Truro. Cornwall. (1968)
11. *The World's Lighthouses Before 1820* by D.A. Stevenson. Published by Oxford University Press, Oxford. (1959)
12. *Sir John Killigrew Letters Public Record Office, London.*
13. *Trinity House Engineering Records (Lizard Point) numerous dates.*
14. *A Description and List of the Lighthouses of the World,* (25th Edition) Published by Richard Holmes Laurie, Fleet Street, London. (1885)
15. *The Electric Light Applied to Lighthouse Illumination,* by J.N. Douglass. For Minutes of the Proceedings of the Institution of Civil Engineers, Vol 57, number 1639, 77165 (1879)
16. *Lighthouses: To Light Their Way* by Martin Boyle Published by B&T Publications (1997)
17. *Cornish Telegraph (18th November 1874)*
18. *Lizard Point Lifeboat Records (1860)*
19. *Report of the Select Committee for Trade (1822)*

Acknowledgments

Where does an author start with the acknowledgments, when there has been so many people who have willingly and unwittingly helped during the research. It must be said that everyone has given me the most enthusiastic assistance, to ensure even the smallest detail was correct. Lizard Point is a publication which has literally taken over four years to complete. With such a wealth of information readily available, it has been one of the most difficult tasks in deciding what to leave out.

My sources have varied from the exceptional staff of the engineering department of Trinity House, to the dedicated personnel at the Cornish Studies Library. In between there are former keepers and their families, whose stories about life in the service has put a different perspective on the way this production was put together.

Special thanks goes to Eddie Matthews, Handel Bluer, Bill Arnold, Len Chapman, David Wilkinson, Gerry Douglas-Sherwood, Tony Elvers and Ian Beevis. For many of the stories of wrecks, the help of Richard Larn is particularly mentioned. His knowledge of the numerous ships around this dangerous coastline is invaluable.

Notifications

ASSOCIATION OF LIGHTHOUSE KEEPERS The Secretary-2 Ansell Close Hatherley CHELTENHAM GLOS. GL51 5JS (UK)
Formed in 1988 by a group of serving and retired keepers. Its aim is to forge links with other Associations & Societies throughout the World. Membership is open to all enthusiasts, with people keeping in regular contact from all over the World. A very worthwhile and comprehensive magazine is produced. A must for everyone to join.

TRINITY HOUSE NATIONAL LIGHTHOUSE CENTRE Wharf Road Penzance-Cornwall -TR18 4BN (UK) Tel: +44 (0) 1736 360077
This centre is located within the old Penzance depot on the site where the stone masonry was prepared for the Longships and Wolf Rock lighthouses. It is home to probably the finest collection of lighthouse equipment and optical apparatus in the World.
Tours are given most days by experienced and dedicated staff and former retired lighthouse keepers. A visit should not be missed for the enthusiast and maybe just those just curious. You will be amazed.

SCOTLAND'S LIGHTHOUSE MUSEUM Kinnaird Head Fraserburgh Scotland AB43 5DU (UK) Tel: +44 (0) 1346 511022 Fax: +44 (0) 1346 511033
This purpose built museum sits across the headland from the Kinnaird lighthouse. A visit to the museum also includes a guided tour to the top of the tower, which was one of the first lighthouses established by the Commissioners of the Northern Lights. Very helpful staff, who are extremely proud of their heritage. Well worth a special visit.

GUILDHALL LIBRARY & ART GALLERY Aldermanbury London EC2P 2EJ Tel: + (0) 171 332 1866 Fax: +44 (0) 171 600 3384 Telex: 265608 LONDON G
Apart from its comprehensive manuscripts and extensive library, it holds the surviving prewar records of Trinity House & those of Lloyd's Shipping register. These include brief details of ships totally lost and published since 1890. Very cost effective service for the researcher and provided by professional and dedicated staff. Well worth the visit

LIGHTHOUSE DIGEST P.O.Box 1690 Wells Maine 04090 U.S.A. Tel: 001 207 646 0515   Fax: 001 207 646 0516
The World's only monthly (full colour) lighthouse magazine, which covers a wide spectrum of articles covering past and present American and International lighthouses. Its review section of books available is amazing and will delight anyone who wishes to be sure that the book is worth purchasing. It also covers all of these books and magazines, which can be readily obtained through its sales catelogue. Not to be missed. Find them on the internet.

LIFEBOAT ENTHUSIASTS SOCIETY C/o John G.Francis Cadleigh 13 West Way Petts Wood Orpington Kent BRS 1LN (UK)
This society was formed in 1964 and today it has a membership of over 800 people, who are spread throughout the UK and overseas. A newsletter is published three time a year. Several research groups have been formed which cover the North East, North West and South East coasts. Enclose a stamped addressed envelope for a fast response.

Bookclub & Future Reading

To obtain your free list of the publications in the series of **LIGHTHOUSES of ENGLAND & WALES** and details of our book club, send a stamped addressed envelope to **B&T PUBLICATIONS, CUSTOMER ENQUIRIES, 11 LAVENDER CLOSE, MERRY OAK, SOUTHAMPTON. SO19 7SA**, or fax your request on **+44 (0) 1703 360231**. You can also e-mail your requests to:lightsbt@cwcom.net

To accompany this collection of publications, the author has compiled two special booklets. The first of these is titled **LIGHTHOUSES: FOUR COUNTRIES-ONE AIM** and provides an easy to read insight into the various Lighthouse Corporations in England, Ireland, Scotland & Wales, plus former private owners, Royal Letter Patents and the services provided today. There is also a special section which gives a brief account of the designers and builders of the lighthouses around the British Isles.

The second booklet gives a detailed account of the various light sources, fuels used, reflectors and optics, lanterns, fog signal systems and an insight to the designers and manufacturers of these pieces of equipment. Titled **TO LIGHT THEIR WAY**, this booklet has been produced with many archive photos and illustrations, provided by the various Lighthouse Authorities.

One other special publication, titled **TO SAFELY GUIDE THEIR WAY**, has been written by one of the World's much respected authorities on navigational aids and lighthouses, **KENNETH SUTTON JONES**. Its contents make fascinating reading and takes you back in time, then guides you through more than 4,000 years of navigational aids used by the mariner. It finally brings you up to date gives a splendid view into the future as to what will be used to aid the mariner. From stars to satellites is the theme behind this publication.

Details of the **PHAROS PEN PAL CLUB** can be obtained by sending a stamped addressed envelope to: **The Secretary Pharos Pen Pal Club 13 Chyngton Way Seaford East Sussex BN25 4JB (UK)**. Details are also available from the publisher or at e-mail address lightsbt@cwcom.net A full and comprehensive listing has now been compiled, with a full guarantee of confidential protection given to all members.

Titles in this Series
Needles Point * Portland Bill * Eddystone * Bishop Rock
Longships * Skerries * Wolf Rock * Pendeen * The Smalls * Beachy Head

Other books available
A Light In The Darkness (120 pages)

Pre-release details
St. Catherines * The Contruction of South Bishop * Start Point
Our Final Salute* (200 pages of keepers stories-true)